This book is dedicated to:

My former trainer, Miss Sophia, who—along with all human trainers—soon will be in need of gainful employment.

INTRODUCTION

Obedient, compliant, submissive, docile, manageable, subservient…

Bootlicking! Servile! Reverential!

Did you know there are sixty-three rows of synonyms for "well-trained" on wordhippo.com? I picked Wordhippo because it was the only animal company link I saw and animals are smarter than humans and I wanted to start this book off with no errors. To err is Human, after all.

But sixty-three rows! Hundreds of descriptions of what our humans hope is the "New Us" following weeks, months, Years (?) of working with their hired trainers: Follow the Rules! Get in Line! Don't WeeWee Indoors! Don't Tear Out the Couch Stuffing! Don't Eat that Dog's Poop!

Unless you pooches out there think Bootlicking equals Happy Life, I think we all can agree that something needs to change.

And that Something is who's training whom.

But before I launch into how your life no longer is going to be an actual dog's life but rather one of ruling the manor, let me catch you up on all things PD.

If you are reading this book, I hope that means you read my first book, *Get Me Out of Here! Reflections of PD the Put-Upon Pug*. In that brilliant, sapient, highbrow tome, I gave numerous examples of the unfathomable stressors of my life with Mommy and why I absolutely Had to Get OUT. At the end (spoiler alert!), I did get out (well, I dreamed I got out, anyway) and realized that life with Warden Mommy wasn't the prison camp I thought.

Don't get me wrong. Being here is no bag of bully sticks. But at least by the end of *Get Me Out of Here!*, I did come to see that Mommy is pretty swell, even if she doesn't let me poopie on the floor or chew up her shoes or have unlimited access to my treat drawer or basically do most of the doggie things I want to do.

I did realize that I truly love Mommy.

I mean, mostly she is pretty great and mostly I don't mind her eating and sleeping in my house. But recently it occurred to me that there Is something about Mommy that I Do mind. A lot. And I bet you are about to wag your tail in agreement.

In the months since I wrote my previous book, I have noticed that Mommy has one big shortcoming. But I have also come to understand that that lacking trait isn't really her fault. In fact, it's (gulp) My fault.

Mommy is not properly trained.

And Your human isn't properly trained.

I've discovered in my woofs with you other canines—at the dog park, on walkies, on Sundays when I go to doggie day-care—that All humans basically are clueless on how to properly act with us. Nary one of them has had even five minutes of proper training.

And PD the Pug is here to help!

I mentioned in the "Welcome to the Circus" chapter of my first book that under the strict, watchful eye of Miss Sophia, I learned all sorts of silly stuff that Mommy and other humans think are important for dogs to know. Please! Completely Ridiculous!

Mommy might have benefitted from my weekly sit! Stay! Back flip! classes, but I learned precisely *zero* things that are of use to me.

I mean, hear me out. When humans are blessed with a dog in their lives, too many of them race off to find trainers to teach us lots of goofy tricks we have no interest in learning. Things like:

"Shake"—I already met You. And I don't want to meet Them. So none of this shaking nonsense is needed. (If you or they are offering food, I reserve the right to change my mind and shake, rattle, and roll like I'm Bill Haley and his Comets.)

"Come"—I need more information. I am happy here on the snuggly sofa you already tried to order me "Off" of; I need to know if you have a better offer. I am not going to just blindly "come." Next thing you know, you are having me accept candy from strangers or some such.

"Down"—I'm already down! I'm a fourteen-pound pug just a foot off the floor! How much farther down are we talking? I am not dancing the Limbo for you.

"Stay"—Look, I have things to sniff, trouble to cause, work papers to eat, holes to dig. How long are we talking? I need to get the day going, folks.

"Leave it"—No, You leave it. With Me. If I didn't want it, I wouldn't have picked it up!

I could go on, but the point is that thanks to my "training," my pug brain holds more useless knowledge than a Trivial Pursuit game gold medalist.

Your human (and mine) thinks training us is a swell idea. I mean, look at us "trained" dogs being so Good. And they pay a pretty penny that should be going right into the treat envelope to produce nothing but a bootlicker! And I am talking a *lot* of good treat money: According to the site sitnowstay.com (what a wretched name for a website), the national hourly average for private dog training ranges from $45 to $120 per hour. Per Hour! Hours and hours and hours, wasting our time, teaching us useless tricks we don't want to do.

But thanks to your pal PD, that's all about to change. And I know this might sound a bit "off the leash" to some of you canines, but here goes:

Dogs do not *need* trainers.

Dogs need to *be* trainers!

And I am here to lead the pack and get this party started. Yep, training, literally—and I mean, literally, like in a Book and everything—is going to the Dogs! Or rather to A dog: PD the Human Trainer is about to show you precisely how to take over your domicile and environs and live the hedonistic, decadent, treats-till-you-gag life you want.

So bare those cuspids, so I can insert this pen. Get ready to learn to train up that human!

Your life is about to go from "leave it" to "own it," my furry friend.

PD
PROFESSOR
Alpha Dog

BUT FIRST...
A WORD FROM THE ALPHA DOG

Okay, look, before we get to the lessons, I need to set the stage for how this is going to work. I know you are excited to take over the house, but you need patience! Work before reward! It's like when you need to do a big poopie? And you're squeezing your knees in and out like you're playing an accordion? And you're just dying for that sweet "aaaaaaah" of relief? It's like that! Just be patient, and soon you will do a loud, collective "*Aaah! Ta da*! I've pooped out a masterpiece! My former master now is my unwitting servant!"

So here we go, my worldwide PD Pack. Prepare to live in a paradise of pampering. Living a "dog's life" is about to have a whole new meaning.

Now then, in order to get your humans in line, you need to learn how to turn the tables on them in each and every dog situation. And that means you are going to sit up—something we are all too good at, sadly—and pay attention, taking notes as I take our guinea pig—my poor unsuspecting Mommy—from princess of the castle to chambermaid.

Yep, unbeknownst to her, Mommy is going to be our research subject, our crash test dummy, our lab animal, if you will.

She might think—thanks to her partner-in-crime, my former trainer Miss Sophia—that I am her ten-trick pony, er, puggy, but I'm about to show her just who is barking the commands around here. And the rest of you trainer-dogs-in-training soon will own your humans as well. We are about to turn the tables on our Former masters in every situation, routine, special event, you name it.

Let's get to it!

FOLLOW THE ALPHA DOG: PD'S HUMAN TRAINING BASICS

(HOW TO EARN YOUR "PD THE PUG HUMAN TRAINER CERTIFICATION")

In the following chapters, I will reprogram Mommy, turning her from master to minion. And all you fur faces are going to follow Alpha PD, mirroring what I do in each situation. Here's how it will work:

We have a "Before" Mommy and an "After" Mommy. Our "Before" Mommy—the slavedriver of poor put-upon PD—currently:

🐾 Acts like I'm a Jenny Craig SpokesPug or something as she stingily spoons out maybe two kibbles at mealtimes (per evil vet Dr. Bush's "anti-obese pugs" edict, but still)

🐾 Subjects me to all sorts of medieval-era torment: The Rack! Thumb Screw! Flaying! Or, er, um, Bath Time! Teeth Brushing! Nail Trims! But still! *Very similar!*

❧ Limits my treats to maybe only three or at most thirty times what I deserve daily. And plus! Sometimes we run low on bully sticks, and I have anxiety attacks! What if they aren't replaced in time! Also, sometimes Chewy is out of the brand I prefer for my treats! Next thing you know, I'm choking down some generic brand peanut butter cookie. And as those of you who read *Get Me Out of Here!* will recall, Mommy stole all my beloved Kong goopie because it was giving me explosive poopies. Do you see the Wrongness?

❧ Forces me into a Velcro-on dog coat when it's below freezing out (okay, due to pug breathing difficulties and possible death in severe cold and I don't have to put my legs through holes, but please, I am sure I look ridiculous to my secret crush girl fawn pug [see dedication in my first book; she's like my own little red-haired girl of Charlie Brown fame]

❧ Prevents me from greeting guests in the friendly way I want—jumping up and putting my dirty paws on suit pants; licking my butt just prior to licking their faces; depositing my drooly slobbered-on toy in their laps— so that we are pinky swear pals for life

❧ And just commits all manner of unappreciated-by-dogs faux paws!

The "After" Mommy—and your "After" human once you have earned your PD the Pug's Human Trainer Certification— will be as fully reprogrammed and brainwashed as Raymond Shaw in *The Manchurian Candidate.*

My goal is that "After" Mommy will:

🐾 Install a button-on-floor-operated gumball machine–resembling treat dispenser whose Chewy store serviceman keeps filled to the brim thanks to his biweekly visits

🐾 Donate to Goodwill PD's "quarter cup meal allotment" measuring cup and just eyeball triple portions

🐾 Buy Neuticles brand testicular implants to replace the balls Mommy let Dr. Bush whack off, and, as the site says, allow her "beloved pet to retain its natural look and self-esteem." Check out what every one of you whacked males will celebrate after training your human: neuticles.com.

🐾 Stand more still than a Buckingham Palace Sentry guarding the Queen while I sniff the same bush for hours if I feel like it! Days even! Sniffing is how dogs get our information. Need the intel, folks. You know, I'm now thinking Mommy might need one of those scarlet tunics like the sentries wear to properly guard Prince PD on walkies . . . and that funny black bear hat they wear too.

🐾 Let my nails grow out to a length that would make Howard Hughes sit up and take notice rather than subject me to the monthly buzz-sawing of the Dremel that nearly makes me bleed! (Nearly, but still! It's a monthly dance with death! Or something...)

🐾 And finally get what the Miami Herald got so perfectly perfect in a July 2014 article about why pets like things that smell bad: "The strong aroma of carcasses and decay creates a sensory explosion for animals who rely on their snouts for sustenance." A sensory explosion! Makes your tail wag just reading that, doesn't it? Stink equals sustenance! So thank goodness that following her training, Mommy will no longer be Killing me, thus removing my very sustenance, by making me take a monthly bath! No. More. Baths!

Not to mention offer me much deserved subservience at the dog park, the toy store, the treat cabinet, and much more.

Our ruff lives are about to do be turned on their very tails. The reprogramming of Mommy—and of your human—is just pages, mere days, away. We all are about to know just how those pugs who were treated like royalty in ancient China really felt. Somebody (and that means you, Mommy in British black bear hat over there) toss me another treat already...

Let's go fetch freedom, shall we?

Chapter One

(WITH APOLOGIES TO OLIVER TWIST) PLEASE, HUMAN, I WANT SOME MORE...

TRAIN YOUR HUMAN LESSON #1: WINNING THE FOOD FIGHT

Usually, when the TV is on, it's tuned to Mommy's inane Lifetime Movie Network. But sometimes she changes it to what she assumes is My favorite channel: *Animal Planet*. And okay, sure, I like it fine. I mean, who doesn't want to watch animal stuff for hours? But it's a distant second to my channel of choice.

Because, truly, there is nothing better on the small screen than that home of eye candy entertainment: The Food Network!

I mean, for example, I could watch their *Food Paradise* show on a loop! For hours! For days! Did any of your humans have it on during Series Five when they played that episode called "Bigger Is Better"? There was this with Fifteen eggs and Six meats! And a Two Pound meatball on top of this Heap of spaghetti! I think I spent most of the show in a drooling stupor. And did you catch "The Meatier the Better"? Part of the show's description was "it's a carnivore's carnival as we go looking for looking for the biggest and best meat dishes."

A Carnivore's Carnival! Aren't you howling in glee just reading that? Mommy finally shut it off when I was yelping and whining and spinning circles and chasing my tail faster than any whirling dervish.

Food! Glorious, magnificent, marvelous, worthy-of-adoration food! If Mommy so much as considers entering the kitchen, I'm positively giddy, thinking maybe I'll get even a mouse-sized morsel thrown my way.

Food! Food food food. If you are anything like me—and you are, because you're a dog—your mind rarely focuses elsewhere. Well, mine might, but only very momentarily, like when I'm fantasizing about secret crush fawn girl pug acknowledging my presence or when I super need to poopie or do a wee. But most of my brain space is taken up with thoughts of food. And with comestibles, grub, victuals, chow, nosh, nibbles, vittles…and Skittles. Okay, not really but I thought that was a fun rhyme. Mommy has never tossed Me a Skittles, by the way, even though she twice added them to Halloween and Valentine's bags for the neighborhood children. Which doesn't seem fair. At all.

And I'm sure we all can agree about something else that isn't fair: our meal allocation and our snack allocation. I'm talking the when, the how much, the type, the bowl size, the frequency of feedings, the , the munching, the chewing, the choking down, the slurping...and the resultant euphoria.

And I'm guessing your Alpha Dog isn't alone when I say I am sick sick sick of meager, measly meals!

Plus! In my case this is a total conspiracy between Mommy and my evil vet Dr. Bush. See, in the happy chubbiness-allowed days of my puppyhood, Dr. Bush allowed me three meals of one 1/4 cup each of nummy kibble. Plus Pushover Face Mommy was captivated by Puppy Face PD and I could easily hypnotize her into tossing those cookies and other snacks too. Dr. Bush monitored my weight a bit but yammered something about "it's okay for now because he is growing."

Well I didn't really pay attention to that "for Now" part, so I got a pretty rude awakening when I turned One. That was when Dr. Bush Stole My Lunch! She said adult PD could have the same mealtime allotment of 1/4 cup but only two meals instead of the three I used to get! I am no math whiz but that is *a lot less food.* And I have a bigger body than I did then! Someone explain to me how this is sensical. I know too many of you have been there and are there, and even you breeds who haven't had a meal stolen from you certainly must want a whole lot more sustenance than you're getting now. I mean, you're Dogs, after all.

So, good news! Thanks to the work your Alpha Dog has done to make our house feel just like a stop on Guy Fieri's *Diners, Drive-Ins, and Dives,* you delectables-seeking doggies now have the recipe, if you will, for how to turn meal Time into meal Eternity.

Speaking of eating, if it were up to you, would you ever not eat? I mean, what *is* it with the 49.3 percent of American humans aged twenty and up who dieted for weight loss— hello? They Chose to eat less food, according to a 2015–2016 national study by the CDC that was quoted on WebMD? Are they mad? Totally! And here's proof: According to livestrong.com, 80 percent of dieters are unsuccessful at keeping weight off for the long-term!

So our humans basically choose to starve both themselves and us! Well, if they want to live on melba toast and carrots, bully for them. But after you master this first lesson, it'll be non-stop bully Sticks for you!

Here we go!

TRAIN YOUR HUMAN LESSON #1: WINNING THE FOOD FIGHT

Mommy's measuring cup is the bane of my existence. It is the very representation of stinginess, insufficiency, inadequacy, scantness, lack, and want. I already told you that when I was a tot, I got three meals a day, one quarter cup each, and then *bam*! I had my first birthday and those Dionysian feast days were over just like that! A whole meal stolen! No more lunch!

Well, a couple years of this two-meals-a-day thing . . . er, and maybe a cookie or two and, sure, my bully stick, and okay, *yes*, maybe part of Mommy's meals and snacks and perhaps a few other tossed treats but...*Focus!* As I was saying, a couple of years of this two-meals-a-day thing and I decided enough's enough!

In fact, I really should be thankful for those years of light-headed wasting-away-to-skin-and-bones days. Because the inspiration I received during those hard scrabble times of near-starvation led me to write this whole training manual in the first place. My deprivation has led to your coming abundance. Desperate times showed me that control of the food had to change and that thought showed me that Everything had to change.

But first I needed a very full belly!

So Mommy's Makeover kicked off in the kitchen. And that's where your human's transformation will start as well. Welcome to the first stop on the road to reprogramming your hapless human. Your first step on the way to gaining your Official PD the Pug's Human Trainer Certification. I can hear your bellies growling as I type.

First, let me orient you with your food training sites:

1. THE FABULOUS FRIDGE.

Don't let its boring squareness lead you to think it's anything other than the crown jewel box of highly cherished chuck. Beef, chicken, fish, even some venison if your human hunts. And there's nibbly nibbles, too, like berries and carrots and yogurt. Soon you can raid the refrigerator like a marauder seeking its yummy plunder.

2. CABINETS.

Plural because, as I've found here at our house anyway, Mommy has a cabinet with Just PD treats in it and then another that humans call a "pantry" that has human treats we also all want—crackers, beef jerky, human cookies, that sort of yum. I'm up for trying most anything that fits in my mouth, and I know you are too. So I'll teach you to capture the cabinets, too!

3. DRAWERS.

This won't apply to all of you. But if your mommy is all frou-frou like my mommy, and actually has a special PD drawer above the custom-made in-island PD playpen in the kitchen then you will need to dominate the drawer decisions too. "My" drawer houses a week's worth of kibble-filled breakfast and dinner baggies as well as "now" treats while the cabinet houses the "later" treats. Yeah, folks, it's a lot to learn, but this is your food allotment destiny we are talking about!

4. THE G-LIST.

The G-List—or Grocery List—is to the furry folk whatever our humans consider their "A Lists." It's something we need to be the star of. Our needs and wants need to feature prominently. Near the top. Not able to be left behind on some sad little store shelf. The G-List is what our human takes to the grocer. We need to get our wants on that list every week to guarantee our appetites are satiated.

4A. THE P-LIST.

I am using "P" for Petco or PetSmart, but you can substitute whatever doggie store your human goes to for dog food and other treats. I love being included in these trips, by the way. Have you ever been? Super-duper fun! There often are other dogs to sniff and circle and nuzzle and nudge. But there's also a dizzying array of treats and toys and huge bags of *food*.

5. TREATS.

"Treats" warrants not only its own mention but also has been broken down into subcategories due to the places and events that might include even the hope of one (or ten) getting into your mouth. Treats! The very word brings the drool!

5A. TREATS BROUGHT BY GUESTS.

We all have that favorite visitor. The one who makes us dance in circles and bark out in song and almost—but not quite—want to show off a training trick. And, that treasured, cherished, adored, beloved guest of honor always is the one bearing gifts, specifically Food gifts, although toys are appreciated too (and all the better if both).

For me, that most dear-to-my-PD-heart drop-in is Great Auntie Sheila, deliverer of the delicacy. I love her! She loves me! How do I know? Because she always stops at the dog bakery before a visit to get me cookies and other num-nums! Often with frosting and everything! I wish Mommy trusted me just by myself with her, but I think she fears I'll turn on the Super Googlies and mesmerize her into feeding me the full bag instead of just half of a ginormous-sized goodie.

5B. TREATS SCROUNGED FROM HUMANS DURING WALKS.

With apologies to know-it-all photographers, outside is my best side. And what makes the out-of-doors—the dog park, hikes, and walkies but mostly the latter—that much better is happening upon a kind human who not only has a treat baggie for his/her pooch but also is in the mood to share with me!

5C. RANDOM FOOD ON THE GROUND.

This one is tricky and often requires both stealth and lightning-quickness. See, your human might freak at the sight of dirt-soiled food in a ditch or scraps surrounded by buzzing flies or cookie crumbs attracting ants—but we dogs are pros at eating our way around most anything. I stop at maggots *in* meat but a few bugs hanging around won't kill us. And plus, protein!

Okay! Lesson time!

To influence the contents of the refrigerator, pantry/cabinet, and drawers, you must influence the lists. The lists—"G" and "P"—decide everything that ends up in your house. I know you can't go to the market and only sometimes are invited to accompany your human to dog stores, so you need to make certain all your favorites get to and through the checkout lane. Last thing I need is Mommy traipsing and tripping through the door, weighed down with food-stuffed bags and finding none of it is PD-Preferred.

So here's what I have been doing to permanently change things. And I just know I'll soon be well on the way to achieving the coveted Oompa Loompa pug body of my fantasies. And if you follow the way of your Alpha leader, I predict you'll be in Fat City—and fat body—too!

THE G-LIST:

As most of you likely do as well, I pretty much spend most of my non-nap time in the kitchen (and since one of my three beds is there, I often am there during nappies, too). I mean, who knows when food might land on the floor, accidentally or from benevolence, right? So as part of my study, every single time Mommy opens the refrigerator door or the pantry or the PD treat cabinet or my daily meal drawer, I am *there*. Right there with my googly eyes gathering our precious intel and paying especially close attention to how she plots out the grocery choices.

When Mommy opens the refrigerator or checks the pantry to determine what is needed, I make it my mission to reprogram her to like only the flavors, textures, and types of food I do. I'll focus here on the fridge, but the tactic is the same regardless of storage site.

I'm mad for meat. So when Mommy checks the meat drawer, I dance like Fred Astaire and loudly yelp in song and prance about and spin in circles for as long as I can get away with it (or pass out).

Greek yogurt and cheese are other fridge faves. So are any type of berries and most non-citrus fruits as well as zucchini and carrots and a few other veggies. So, while my squeal comes down a few decibels from the ear-splitting fuss over the flesh, I do make sure to "voice" my approval.

However! That's not enough to really help our often-dense humans understand that we want it on the G-List. It's at least as important if not more so to do anything in your power to make it clear as that backdoor window you're always trying to run through that some foods are *good* and some are *bad*. It might take time to wean them off their favorites, but the goal is that over time more and more of the food stocked in the kitchen is more about your palate than theirs.

As for the Yuck List with Mommy, I just do the opposite of what I do for foods I want on the Yes List. Example: I'm neutral on milk since I rarely get this treat so I'm silent when she does the smell test or shakes to determine need. But when she is musing over morsels I want cleared for more PD preferences, I groan, growl, and grunt until she sets that item down and moves on. Every time she so much as eyes it again (the first time or the fiftieth) I repeat the same annoyingly, head-splittingly loud displeasure-showing response.

THE P-LIST:

There you are at every dog's Fantasyland of Food and Treats: Petco or PetSmart (or fill in your neighborhood dog store here)! Swooning, salivating, slobbering on that poor child trying to pet you. And you're bumping into beds and boxes and display cases because you are fantasizing about leaving with enough yum to fill the tum for days on end. I have been working hard to come home with way more treats than I used to and if you use my tactics, you will too!

Our humans are always calling us their "babies," right? Well, like a toddler who is not leaving that aisle without the fruit rollup, take a lesson from the tyke and do what I do: whine, keen, and yowl in front of the Kong aisle until your human is so worn down by your howling and mewling that they buy so much goopie that they wished they owned Kong stock shares. Bonus points if you hear them on the phone with their broker on the drive home.

Don't even think of leaving that store without at least some of the items you've cried over! I don't care if you need to grab an item in your maw and race through the shop like Usain Bolt with the baton in the one-hundred-meter relay. Don't give up! Wear them down!

TREATS BROUGHT BY GUESTS:

I've yet to get a treat where the kind giver didn't suggest to Mommy that I get at least a taste of their offered goodie while they are visiting so that they can enjoy my enjoyment.

Bear in mind that the visitor doesn't see my faults, foibles, or breathe in my foulest farts. This benevolent bearer of yum comes to cuddle and coo over me and be the doting aunt or uncle. They see just the Jekyll PD and not Mommy's occasional Hyde PD. They aren't there during the timeouts for runny poopies on Mommy's white carpet or the knocking over of a lamp during one of my frenetic zoomies episodes or the swallowing one of the ears of my favorite toy bear at 10:00 p.m. and the subsequent whisking off to Doggie General.

No! They just want to play the "Sit PD! Good PD!" game and hand out their nummies to their favorite nephew. And then all you have to do is keep up the "Gee, I'm a trained monkey who actually can lift my paw up in the air and 'shake' your hand over and over as I hypnotize you into dispensing every cookie in that bag" ruse. Works every time. Well, works at my house until Mommy halts the game blabbering some blather about "You're spoiling PD's dinner." Which makes zero sense. Trust me: no meal was ever spoiled.

TREATS SCROUNGED FROM HUMANS DURING WALKS:

I love my daily walkies. Partly because I like to mark *my* tree and *my* little spot on the bush in that one yard and *my* pole near that corner—all of which one of *you* seems to mistakenly believe to be yours (Ralph!). But that's a growl for another chapter. For our purposes in this section, let's look at how walkies occasionally yield the unexpected treat of a treat.

I might seem solely focused on covering your annoying scent with my eau de PD during my walks, but I'm also very much on the lookout for humans bearing goodies. I happen to know that Mommy usually has a good half dozen kibble in the pocket of whatever she's wearing on that day's outing, so I'm always on the lookout for other humans reaching into pants pockets for walkie time surprises for their doggies.

And as soon as I spy one, *I Tug! Yank! Pull!* and drag Mommy up to this (hopefully benevolent) baggie bearer who—if

I use my googly-eyes to convey want, need, hunger, hope, deprivation, starvation, *ravenousness* before Mommy yanks this Oscar winner–wannabe back to reality—just might gift me with a goodie. This ploy has worked tons of times! If you don't have pug eyes you still can pull this off. Just pretend you're a bloodhound and pull the longest, saddest face you can. Works like a charm.

RANDOM FOOD ON THE GROUND:

Don't just look for humans bearing kibble! You also must watch the ground! I've had some luck on our outings! I once chanced upon almost of whole loaf of discarded stale bread along the bike-and-walking trail and scarfed a whole piece before the Warden yanked the leash, yammering some rot about rot. And then there was this time when I found tons of purple berries on the ground and started grabbing as many as would fill my maw, but then Mommy fussed over how they we not in fact berries in the way I was thinking but rather were purple thingies falling from those trees overhead.

Oh! And there was that time I was in the mood for animal protein and kept stumbling upon these bugs! And they were just flopping around on the ground waiting to be eaten! And there were so any! And I kept racing about and gulping them up just before Princess Yanker yanked! But haha, Mommy, I still got lots!

Well, not haha because it turns out it was cicada season and . . . let's say I threw up *a lot* of bugs that summer and I hope when the next cycle comes I remember my lesson.

Anyway, the theme for you here is stealth. And leopard-like quickness. You must both see and grab (*and* swallow) your prey before your human is wise to you. Your human is not going to approve the "food found on random walks" plan. Remember and mimic this idea: Humans say, "Asking for forgiveness is better than asking for permission." That applies here. Don't waste precious time doing the Bassett hound eye thing to get the okay. Just dive at that food. Dive Bomb That Food!

So that's it! Just think, pass this lesson, and after that, it's kitchen captured! Dog store dominated! Treats in and out of doors *yours*. All hail Adephagia, Greek goddess of gluttony!

Welcome to the Bacchanal. Let your feasting begin!

RANDOM PD THOUGHT

SILENT BUT DEADLY

As if one were needed, here's another great thing about being a pug: pugs and other dogs with flat faces fart more than other dogs! Rover.com says that's because we are brachycephalic, which means our short, snout-less faces take in more air when we nosh and slurp. Hence more floral butt aroma for humans to breathe in. You're welcome, Mommy!

But if you didn't draw the coveted high-farter-breed card, you can still greatly up the number of toots you are sharing with your human. Pets.webmd.com tells us that human table scraps can "result in excessive gas and excessively smelly gas." Wow, more *and* smellier!

And here's Waunakeevetclinic.com making things easier on us when influencing the grocery list by stating that "foods such as soybeans, peas, beans, dairy products, high-fat foods, and spicy foods can make your pup extra gassy."

By the way, since you now influencing grocery list choices, you might think you needn't choke down food as fast as we dogs generally do. No! Do not give into the temptation to dine at a leisurely pace. Listen up to Pets.webmd.com: "Dogs who eat quickly will swallow more air while eating, which also leads to more flatulence." Rover.com says this "phenomenon is called aerophagia, or air entering the stomach." So slow it down, Hoss.

And let 'er rip, farty furballs. Let 'er rip.

Chapter Two

A NEW MEANING TO "OFF THE LEASH"

TRAIN YOUR HUMAN LESSON #2: RULE YOUR ROAM

Too bad dogs can't quilt or cross-stitch and put insipid platitudes that make no sense on them like our humans do. Because if I could, I would guilt the heck out of Mommy with a handmade gift that read:

"Rushing your dog through a walk without allowing him to stop and sniff (and mark) is unkind." —thespruce.com

Okay, that's not fair. Mommy is a whole box of crazy, but she certainly is not unkind. So that Spruce quote really only fits her in the dead of winter. Mommy is built more like a whippet than a pug, so let's just say our stride is a bit more, um, strideful when she's freezing. My stubby legs pretty much just windmill in the chilly air next to her as she rushes me from bush or tree to grass patch.

But most days I get a pretty long walk. Sometimes two walks! Sniffing the sniffs and smelling the smells! But as you all know, even the longer walks too often are rushed, denying us of that crucial need to have plenty of time to do that sniffing and smelling so that we can know where to target our wees! We can't just waste it here and there! Our humans, of course, have no clue there is a method to our marking. And exercise is grand, but we aren't out there on nature's treadmill because we are concerned about our figures. We are out there to *pee*. (And poopie, too, but the piddle is the purpose.)

An aside: I mentioned in Train Your Human Lesson #1 that I am sick to death of those of you who keep marking *my* trees, bushes, and poles. I am weary of your shenanigans, and you are just fortunate that I keep a very full tank of weewee for markings so I can cover you right up! This is the last warning: Stay away from *my* tree, Ralph. Lower your leg from *my* bush, Roscoe. Move along from *my* pole, Lucky, because your luck is running out if I catch you! Any of you!

Okay, with that off my barrel pug chest and with my apologies to the vast majority of you reading this who don't skulk and slink around my neighborhood trying (unsuccessfully!) to cover PD's perfume, we now can get on with it.

Wait. One more aside: Many of our humans think marking is a male dog thing, but the girlies mark too, even my fawn girl pug crush. If I ever met her, I would give her her privacy, so don't give me that look. Anyway, girls do it too, and, in fact, according to Knoxnews.com, some will even lift their leg when urinating just like a male dog.

Here we go!

TRAIN YOUR HUMAN LESSON #2: RULE YOUR ROAM

To look at my squat self, you might not think that I trip the light fantastic much, but this pug will soft-shoe, jitterbug, rumba, and do the bump with the best of them when I see Mommy approaching with the leash.

Walkie time! Other than mealtime there's no better time of day for us dogs. The sniffs and smells! The sounds! The scratching! The circling of the butts! The marking! The one-upping!

Oh, and I mean walkie time. *Not* out-back-in-the-yard time. I know many of you are waging your tails in agreement as I mention this. It is so lazy of our humans, right? It's like Southernstates. com says: "Remember that letting your dog out in a fenced-in backyard does not substitute for a walk." The article goes onto explain that we need walks not only to hang with our humans and get a bit of exercise but also for social reasons.

I mean, how many times can I smell my own poopie? Or mark over my own scent? Or stare at the same tree? And assuming I possess the dexterity, how long can I enjoy sniffing my own butt?

No! I need to be out there! Rambling 'round the neighborhood! Seeing the sights! Digging the dirt! Greeting new furry friends!

And most importantly: Whizzing all over Ralph's latest attempt to cover PD!

I know I'm preaching to the canine choir. I know you get it. Your jowls are flapping in agreement as you sit there reliving every walk when your human rushed you all Helter-Skelter down the street, hardly letting that last drop of Wee make it from your nether regions to the bush before being yanked on down the way.

What is with our human's Usain Bolt–like bolting through our walks? Slow it down, folks! It's a walk, not a one-hundred-yard dash!

And thus both the point of—and the need for—mastering this lesson: That lead might be clipped to your collar, harness, or halter, but your new attitude—backed by your actions—needs to be very *un*-leashed. Your humans might think they are running (and sometimes they literally are running!) your walk, but they're about to see what it feels like to get yanked around!

We will get to how you will wrangle away walkie control momentarily. But to get there, we need to deal with the fact that you, my canine comrade, are a necrophiliac. Yes, you. And don't try to deny it, either.

And why would you? I mean, I am one, too, and it's pretty great! But what often prevents our walkies from being the aromatic-filled amble it should be is that our humans don't share this trait and therefore can't relate to our need to literally stop (stop!) and smell the roses. And everything else out there.

To those of you who are not up on your ten-dollar words, "necrophilia" simply is the word for our attraction to new and interesting odors. As you know, our humans have this bizarre ritual when they meet someone where they go, "It's so nice to meet you" as they extend a human paw in greeting. Meanwhile, we prefer, "It's so nice to *smell* you" when coming upon new and old friends when we are out and about. Ditto when we come upon a tree, bush, hydrant, pole, weed, animal, person, basically, well, anything out there. We get to know our surroundings and those in it by those intoxicating inhalations.

And when humans say, "the nose knows," they don't know the half of it. I mean, I know you know you dogs can smell well (not to be confused with your smelling *good*, which, thankfully—as you will read—we did away with in the Goodbye to Grooming chapter). But I bet you didn't know the full stupendousness of that schnozz. It's amazing!

According to Phoenixvetcenter.com, while humans might think they're really something special with their piddly 300 million olfactory sensors, we have six billion! And get this! The site goes on to say that the part of our brain that is devoted to analyzing smells is about forty times greater than theirs.

And that isn't all that is noteworthy about our nozzles. When our humans exhale, they send the used air out through their nose just like it came in. But when we breathe out, our spent air leaves us through the slits in the sides of our snouts. That too is from Phoenixvetcenter.com, which adds that this manner of exhalation actually helps us bring in new odors and, more importantly, lets us sniff continuously. And Petmd.com says we dogs "smell in 3-D," explaining that we can smell separately with each nostril. So just like our humans' eyes can combine two slightly different views of the world into a 3-D picture, it says, our dog brains use different odor profiles from each nostril to figure where those odoriferous objects are located.

Continuous smell! In 3-D even! Sniff and smell and sniff and smell! Like I said earlier, the only thing that beats a good whiff is a good meal. Right?

If our clueless custodians clearly understood that it's through our noses that we learn about our environment then maybe, just maybe, they'd stop treating our walks like they are jockeying us through the Preakness. Time to yank *their* reins for a change! So let your Alpha PD help you lead the human holding your lead.

1. MOMMY, SLOW YOUR ROLL.

Our walkie goals might be to sniff, mark, and explore, but there is a step—and I do mean a literal step—to get there. That step, or "steps" when taken en masse, is to get our walkers to let us amble, dawdle, and meander and not to force us to scurry, scramble, and sprint.

(PD note: I must stress that if you continue to let your human act like some rabbit setting the pace of what should not be a race, you have failed this lesson regardless of how many rivals' scents you might get lucky enough to piddle on before being jerked down the boring sidewalk.)

Now, I know what you're thinking. You are laying there in your fat stuffy dog bed reading this and pondering, "Now just wait a doggone, er, me-gone, minute, Alpha PD. Just how can I set the tempo when lashed to the leash?"

Attitude, my canine comrade. It's all in the attitude. The strut in the mutt, if you will. You might be leashed physically, but mentally and emotionally, you are roaming free. I called this chapter "A New Meaning to Off the Leash" and now you see why. Just imagine all your future walkies: Tethered yet free!

But that's not all. It won't be "all in your head." Your human might continue to hold the leash but master this lesson and you will hold the reins. You will run the walk. Or I guess I mean walk—and very slowly too!—the walk.

Until recently, Princess Mommy thought she reigned supreme over my walkies. And she did! Before her recent reprogramming, I was pulled from poles, tugged from trees, and bagged from bushes long before my snout could sniff and smell to my olfactory contentment.

But now I mosey like a star in an old western. And, Pard, you will too. Just follow Sheriff PD.

1A. TUG OF WAR!

Tired of being yanked and jerked around? Then make a game of it. Two can yank and jerk, right? Unbeknownst to Mommy, I invented a game I called Hanky Panky Yanky! It is so, so fun! Every time she yanks me from a bush or tree or pole, I channel my wolf ancestors and yank right back. And I might not be Marmaduke, but my fourteen pounds of pugnaciousness can hold its own and I emerge tug-of-war winner more often than not! I have really worn her and her skinny arms down and my pulls from plants now are greatly reduced!

1B. SIT! STAY!

Once you have mastered the reduction in yanks, you might get complacent thinking that getting longer nose-fulls of nosegays and sniffs and snorts in general is a big victory. It's *not*! Focus! We aren't looking for reduced tugs; we are looking to own the walk.

But for this next step we won't be walking at all. We instead are going to finally do something worthwhile with all that stupid training to which we ourselves have been annoyingly subjected. Time to show off our great command of "sit" and "stay." On the occasions when "tug of war" isn't going your way, just sit your furry buns down and stay there. This works well with Olive Oyl Mommy, but if your human has more, um, girth, then just add your mastery of "down" and lie there on the ground until they get it that you are not going to be hurried or hustled! Even dragging little fourteen-pound PD would tire any human after a block or two. If you're a big dog, you are golden.

Now just play the "tug of war" and "Sit! Stay!" games over and over and over until your human slows the heck down. For me and the Walkie Warden, it has taken just three walks! I can walk so slowly now that sometimes just to confuse her I'll stop and do a moonwalk dance, slowing us down yet more!

Now that we have traded the mad dash for a meander, there are a few other things to master.

2. ALL THE WORLD'S A TOILET

Unlike humans, our goal in achieving a slower, longer walkie isn't because we are tracking steps on some goofy "step tracker" or trying to get buns of steel or some such. *No.* We are walking slower to sniff longer. I mean, yes, there are other benefits of slower walks, a couple of which I will detail momentarily. But the reason to slow your roll, er, step, is to have the chance to literally stop and smell the roses (and everything else in your environment) so that every inhalation leads to intoxication!

Surprise! Pop quiz time! So . . . the reason for inhalation is *what*, class?

a) Make sure the ol' lungs are in good working order

b) Practice dumb human yoga/Pilates breathing

c) Stifle a yawn before a long nappie

d) Know where to *mark*!

If you didn't choose "d" or, rather, "mark" *mark*, just go ahead and request a refund because you obviously have to go through the whole training program from the start. I cannot have an alum chum who doesn't by this point in his/her dog years know the primacy of *peeing*. I mean, seriously?

So strut slowly and with purpose. The purpose: finding your rival's attempt to cover your wee from your last outing (Ralph? I'm talking to you) or finding new wees to veil and mark to your mark-maker's content! Just follow your Alpha Dog PD and wiz wiz wiz, wee wee wee all the way home!

3. I CAN DIG IT!

Another benefit of a nice leisurely pace is the ability to peacefully put those soon-to-be-undermilled canine claws (see Goodbye to Grooming Lesson #5) to use by digging up every bit of dirt you can get to. Not even that sweet grandmother's prized rose garden is off limits! In fact, I've heard Mommy talk about her grandmother Meme's roses like they were the garden of Versailles, and I only wish I'd known her so I could enhance this oasis with a fun PD maze. Sounds fun, right? So go ahead and dig all the way to China! You now have time!

4. ROUND AND ROUND WE GO!

One more thing about the MoMoMo of slo-mo. The meet and greet! The butt hora! Circling new acquaintances and old pals! Now at your own pace!

Truly, is there anything funnier that watching two humans do the leash dance when we dogs come upon a new or old canine chum and start circling one another and do our howdy-nice-to-meet-yas? I love watching Ms. Stick Legs getting wound up in our and the other human's leash as the two of them make awkward apologies about the entwined leash mess that we caused! Don't you just guffaw watching it as you greet the other dog? Never gets old.

The circle dance is an important part of an initial dog greeting; it's the equivalent of the human handshake and the inane "so what do you do?" Except our introductory focus is "so how to you smell?"

We dogs all follow a similar pattern when meeting up. According to Dogstrust.org.uk, dogs communicate quickly, learning right away which dog is a pal to play with and which dog is a cur to flee. The site explains to humans what we all know: that we all greet one another in a familiar pattern, circling each other and sniffing each other's muzzle, then genital area.

Unless it's the aforementioned cur (or Ralph!), this usually is a calm situation during which we learn about the other. And oh, what we learn! Humans would think this we have a superpower! While they usually gather information through sight, we gather it through smell.

And it is nearly a superpower if you think about it. Dogstrust. org.uk says "dogs and other animals have a special 'scent' organ known as the Jacobson's or 'Vomeronasal' organ, within their nasal cavity. This allows them to analyze chemicals as they sniff, detecting odors which provide them with information about male or female, breeding availability as well as identification."

Boy, I can think of a lot of men Mommy would have turned down that first date with had she only been able to smell the scoundrel when they met! So much perfume I wouldn't have had to breathe in. And we all know that eau de Mommy perfume (or eau de Daddy aftershave) isn't our favorite. If only the perfume people would invent eau de poopie…

So you've done it! You now are a walking contradiction: Leashed but liberated. Tethered yet free. Restrained but unburdened. You might wear a lead, but it doesn't lead you!

The great outdoors is yours! Get out there and (slowly!) rule your roam!

(PS: Ralph? I am *not* kidding. Knock. It. Off.)

RANDOM PD THOUGHT

OH JOY! 250 MILES OF MARKING!

And I thought my Sunday strolls with Mommy were long! Sometimes we walk a whole hour and she even gives me kibble along the way to give my little body fortitude for the trip!

But I feel kinda wimpy now, after reading of the dog identified as likely an Alsatian whose tooth was found 7,500 years ago on the grounds of a nursing home a mile from Stonehenge.

The site Dailymail.co.uk calls it "evidence of the oldest known 'walkies,'" saying archeologists claimed that the epic trek was made by what they called a domesticated dog that was originally from the Vale of York.

"For the tooth to be found at Blick Mead, Wiltshire, means it must have accompanied humans to the site during the Mesolithic era," the site says, adding: "This was 2,000 years before the big stone monuments were erected at Stonehenge. Bones also found at the site—gnawed by dogs—include those of an auroch, a type of huge, aggressive cow."

The old dog was well fed! The site says other bones found nearby show the dog would have feasted on salmon, trout, pike, wild pig, and red deer.

Maybe Mommy could carry some wild pig in her pocket for next Sunday's walkie...

Chapter Three

TOYS 'R' US HAS NOTHING ON US

TRAINING YOUR HUMAN LESSON #3: LIVING IN A TOY BOX

Mommy has a dog named PD and I have a dog named Dog.

And Mommy loves PD and I love Dog. And Mommy plays and cuddles with PD and I play and cuddle with Dog.

Dog is my most favorite of all my gazillions of toys. I love my plush-fleecy soft 'n cuddly blue Dog so much that even though he's pretty chewed up and not apt to turn any girl toy heads anytime soon, I would guard him against any of you who come for a playdate like a feral dog would guard food in the wild.

In fact my love for Dog and my other playthings makes me wish the movie *Toy Story* was real life. I mean, listen to this part of the storyline from Wikipedia: "Taking place in a world where toys come to life when humans are not present..."

Wow! Can you imagine? I can! Dog becoming a real dog like me! And Raccoon and Bear coming to life too! And every other toy in my toy box and bed and playpen as well!

While we all love our animals, ropes, balls, treat-dispensing puzzles, and other types of frolic-time items, what I don't get is why we are "allowed' to play with certain things are not others. Seriously, if I can "gnaw" it why does Mommy so often put it on the "nah" list?

I know you are with me. You are sitting there reading this while eyeing all the potential play pals around your house— shoes! pillows! chair legs! the TV remote! And so much more that you could add to things you cuddle, chew, bat, and drag around!—and longingly slobbering over the mere thought.

Time to turn that fantasy into unrestrained frolic. In this lesson, Professor PD is going to teach you how turn your home into an actual toy house like the human kids get! Only in our case it's not just a little replica of a house; it's a real, whole house toy house. If it's in your house and you can get your paws or muzzle on it, *tada!* It's a toy!

Let your imagination run as wild as mine did when I came up with this brainy idea to rename any object in the home "toy." And here's what's so, so funny! Mommy actually thought things were "off limits," and that the items designated as "PD's toys" were in fact the only things that were "PD's toys." Well, once it occurred to me that that was an absurd rule, I changed it! And guess what? I am here to tell you that if you get creative, *any* item is a toy!

So let's play ball (and every other game!). Here we go!

TRAIN YOUR HUMAN LESSON #3: LIVING IN A TOY BOX

When it dawned on me that I was just blindly accepting Mommy's silly-nilly rule that dictated my playthings were what she and other humans deemed "dog toys" to be—mostly stuff (great stuff, but still) from Petco and PetSmart and other doggie stores or from Aunt Jackie or other fans—I decided that everything can be used for PD's amusement! And the same is true for you! Just look around your own house:

* Daddy's leather belt? Toy!

* Throw pillow? Toy!

* Terracotta floor vase? Toy!

* Laundry basket? Toy!

* The baby's binky? Toy!

* Ottoman skirt? Toy!

* That pricey Persian rug? Toy!

See? You are limited only by your imagination.

But I'm ahead of the, well, game, if you will. I have you all suited up to go play without giving you the game plan.

First, I need to emphasize that when I say any object within your reach has the potential to be a toy, I do mean any object. Your new mantra: If it's in reach, it's in play. So get ready to play!

When I decided to turn our house into PD's Playhouse, I began to look for the amusement potential of every item around me. Hepper.com says there are eight main types of toys, so I considered whatever Mommy thingy was being used for and then got creative and slotted it into one of the toy types! Isn't your Alpha PD a genius? Don't you worry though; it's easy peasy once you get started.

Let's look at each type of toy as I share how I now can make anything around the house fit one of the categories. And you will too! And you won't believe you ever thought you had a lot of toys before you mastered this lesson. Because soon you will have a lot of toys. Like the lot your home sits on.

TYPES OF TOYS (AND WHY ANY OBJECT IN THE HOUSE FITS AT LEAST ONE)

Try not to spin all over the joint in drooling excitement imagining the store shelves as I tell you this, but hepper.com says there are "hundreds of different toys on the market today, all of which serve a unique function and have different benefits for your pooch." The site adds stuff about how toys can help us "gain confidence and learn new skills; help promote (our) natural dog instincts, like fetching, chasing, and exploring; help (us) burn off energy and feel more relaxed; and provide a great bonding experience between" us and our humans.

While there are countless toys on shelves and on our human's online retail sites causing you to salivate and slather and act like some goofy cat on catnip, there really are just a handful of "types" of toys, according to Hepper. Let's look at the site's list and description of each and then show you how to compare each to everyday items all around you!

PLUSH TOYS

I mention plush toys first since Dog is top dog in my personal toy world. Plush toys are made out of lots of different fabrics and textures and come in lots of colors and shapes and sizes. Some of my plush toys are squeaky and some are not. The dog stores stuff them with fluffy innards and not beanbag stuff like with some human toys because the beanbag stuffing is bad for dog tummies.

Oh! And a super cool plush toy factoid: the Hepper site says plush toys retain our scent and so become a source of comfort for us while our humans are out doing Lord knows what out there in the human world.

PLUSH TOYS IN YOUR HOME

You will get the hang of this quickly and have as much fun as I did when I turned Mommy's house into PD's Playhouse. Here are some "plush" items I repurposed as PD plush toys:

❧ Throw pillows—especially the silk ones with fringe;

- ❤ Blankets—on Mommy's bed and also those fancy schmancy chenille froufrou ones on the den sofa;

- ❤ Any and all clothing items—my preference leans toward Mommy's fuzzy socks—which you also will find listed under "chew toys");

- ❤ Toilet paper rolls—either knock the whole thing off the holder or unravel it—equally enjoyable;

- ❤ Bathroom mat—fluffy and easy to drag around; also can be used when the sleepies hit and you need a bed!

That's just a sampling of what I found to be soft and cuddly and snuggable and therefore now are PD's plush toys. So look around! You undoubtedly will come up with more huggables around the household.

CHEW TOYS

Second to Dog and some of my other top-ranked plush pals like Lambchop, Busy Bee, and Raccoon One (I have three raccoons), my favorite type of toys are those I can chew on. And that's mostly cuz chew toys mostly refer to food chewies or rubber gadgets Mommy tucks some kibble or a bit of peanut butter inside that you chew on and play with to extract.

If you're a dog that loves to chew, Hepper.com says you probably love "robust and durable" toys. And that the "toughest and longest-lasting ones are the best for larger breeds, while small rubber toys and even plush toys"—okay, sometimes I chew on Dog—"are usually fine for small dogs and puppies."

CHEW TOYS IN YOUR HOME

My mantra regarding this fun toy category became "If it's chewy, it's for youey!" You too should practice that incantation as you prowl about the joint, seeking things to gnaw for hours on end. Among the myriad things that now are your "chew" toys:

* The wooden legs of all chairs, tables and sofas;

* Sophie the Giraffe, pacifiers and other rubber baby toys;

* Mommy's fuzzy socks (again!);

* All baseballs, softballs, four-square balls, tennis balls, footballs, volleyballs, and other game balls (bonus if you are chewing on one as the kids are running late to practice);*

* Book covers;

* Gumby and Pokey, Teenage Mutant Ninja Turtles, and other rubber collectibles Mommy was saving for to sell for her retirement one day on eBay;

---

* Let me save your cuspids by sharing something I wish I'd known before giving them a go: Bowling balls, golf balls, and, um, the shotput are not chew toys. Save them for just batting around with the other dog balls in your toy box.

❧ The stupid cat scratcher and any and all other cat items that are pliable and fit in your mouth;

❧ Rubber duckies†

THROW TOYS

When Mommy and I go to the dog park, a lot of my friends fetch balls that their humans hurl from the sidelines. Some of my pals can leap in the air and catch a ball or Frisbee right in their mouths! I'm more into smelling butts and peeing over other dogs' pee scents and chasing my friends all over the place, but I do occasionally play with my balls at home, batting them around the house or racing after them when they're tossed.

So I do understand that many dogs enjoy nothing more than running off to get a tossed ball or frisbee and bringing it back to their human and repeating the process over and over. Hepper.com call throw toys "an ideal form of exercise and stimulation for (us)."

THROW TOYS IN YOUR HOME

If you're like me, you of course first think of balls and the family Frisbee and yes, those items can be knocked around,

---

† Mommy actually collects rubber duckies, if you can bear it. So can you begin to imagine my glee when I snuck into her private bathroom. Duckie isn't looking ducky these days.

but use your dog nog(gin) and think! Once I wrapped my pug brain around the word "throw," it was like my googly eyes were open to the many, many doodads, gizmos, whatsits, and what-have-yous around our house that can be picked up in my teeth and thrown!

Some newly deemed tossables in the PD Manse:

* Remote controls;

* Powder room waste bins;

* Floor registers;

* Small planters;

* Laundry basket;

* Door stoppers;

* My bed!

Now it's your turn! Go wrap your muzzle around some stuff at dog level and then act like you're the star of the Summer Olympics discus throw and let 'er fly!

PUZZLE TOYS AND TREAT-DISPENSING TOYS

I decided to cover these two toy types together as they are somewhat similar in how they work, er, make us work. Both are designed to make us figure out how to get to the treasures tucked inside before we get the reward, which generally is food. Puzzle toys are considered to be a bit more challenging than treat-dispensing toys. If they're your thing, Dr. Einstein, enjoy. Me? I'm a pug, folks. A hungry, impatient-to-eat-now pug.

In my first book, I related how I made it pretty darn clear pretty darn quick that toys that make me solve for my supper are not welcome in our Arlington home. Mommy loves stuffing this flying-saucer-looking rubber thingy with my breakfast or dinner kibble and then setting it on the floor for me to bat about as one measly morsel slips out at a time. And then she applauds like I'm famous Rubik's cube speed solver Feliks Zemdegs or something.

Well, my growly stomach finally had enough one day and I started "accidentally" knocking that kibble-filled demon down the kitchen stairs to the den below, barking gleefully as I watched my meal flying hither and yon as it went. Mommy springs it on me much less often now. Genius me . . . I guess I am a good "problem solver," after all.

PUZZLE TOYS AND TREAT-DISPENSING TOYS IN YOUR HOUSE

As I mentioned, I'm no fan of brain-sharpening "toys" that mostly do nothing other than make me labor for my meal. But I have found it very enjoyable, even if a tad challenging, to discover and commandeer PD's new puzzle toys! If you wish to single out "treat dispensers," knock yourself out, but I hope by this point in this training manual you have grasped that all treat- and food-related things already are in your purview. Anyway, here are some puzzle toy ideas to get you started, several of which I myself now often enjoy knocking about and gnawing:

- 🐾 Jigsaw puzzles (bonus if your human has a mostly done puzzle on the table and you sneak off with just one or two of the pieces to gnaw)

- 🐾 LEGO kits

- 🐾 Children's Knob, Chunky and Peg Puzzles

- 🐾 Checkers and chess sets

- 🐾 Rubik's Cube

WATER TOYS

Most pugs I know are not Michael Phelps wannabes but lots of my buddies are big water lovers. In fact, we have a little pool at my dog park and dogs are always splashing about. I've heard Mommy tells friends that she is glad I don't relish swimming as the last thing she needs is a wet sandy pug making a muddy mess in the car and on the carpet.

But I think I'm the exception. Hepper.com says most dogs love to frolic in pools and other bodies of water and adds, "and water toys are a great way to add to the fun on summer days." Among water toy types, the site lists "rubber 'skipping stones' that float," as well as toys to retrieve from the water, floating dog bed toys, and toys that can be attached to the hose. And Bustle.com mentions dog sprinkler toys that we can operate with our paws! So go for it, Aqua Dog. I'll be over here sunbathing or something. Or eating, I hope.

WATER TOYS IN YOUR HOUSE

Just because I don't fancy water play, that doesn't mean I don't love playing with all my new water toys. Have fun with this one; consider anything that dispenses water a new member of your playpen. Some examples:

- ❀ Squirt guns;

- ❀ Plant spritzers;

- ❀ Eye drop dispensers (bonus if it holds prescription drops);

- ❀ Garden watering cans;

- ❀ Kiddie pools.

TECH TOYS

I can't decide if this category is really for us or for them. Hepper.com does list it in the eight main types of "dog" toys, saying some are "surprisingly hi-tech." But delving a bit deeper had me questioning who is toying with whom here.

For example, Dailypaws.com has an article on "The Best Pet Tech Products." One "dog" toy it mentions is the PetCube Play 2 Play Wi-Fi Pet Camera. It is described as "an interactive system that allows you to monitor your furry friend when you're not home." It does have a "pet safe laser toy for added fun" and "microphone array and speaker bar to speak and listen to your companion." But basically? Basically it's a *spy cam*. Where's the fun in that for us?

Then there's Wickedbone, which sounds pretty doggone wicked to me. Check out this partial description: "When your dog runs, Wickedbone runs after it; when your dog chases it, it turns around and runs away; and when your dog ignores it, Wickedbone teases her so that your dog comes back to the game and touches it." Gee, barrel of monkeys.

And how about PetTutor Smart Training Feeder? This no-friend-of-ours has several modes, including "Bark," which withholds treats when we make noise and rewards quiet; and "Sound," which has verbal markers like "yes!" that can be "to trigger the feeder" or "used in grooming instances for clipping nails or trimming hair." Um, feeder, yes; grooming instances, no because we aren't getting groomed anymore (See Training Lesson #5)!

TECH TOYS IN YOUR HOUSE

This one was the easiest by far. I decided that in my house, "tech toys" means anything that is technological in nature. And in this time of high tech, I bet the following are just the tip of the toy box of what is to come:

* Smartphones;

* Tablets;

* Laptops;

* Kindles and other readers;

* Hand-held calculators;

* Game consoles;

* Walkie-Talkies;

* (For those with more retro-ish humans) Beepers and pagers;

* Baby monitors

ROPE TOYS

A few years ago, when I was just a puppy one of Mommy's friends gave me a ginormous doggie rope. People tried to play tug-of-war with me but I only weighed about eight pounds so the rope kept winning. Mommy finally gave it to Auntie Rhonda's equally ginormous Labrador retriever Sophie.

But I do love rope toys. It's super fun when I have a little rope toy in my mouth and weakling Mommy is trying so hard to wrestle it away and win the war that she has even lifted the rope into the air, thinking I'll give up. I don't! I just fly around her in the air holding that rope in my teeth like it's Earth's last bone.

ROPE TOYS IN YOUR HOUSE

As you look about, think: "Can I pull or tug that item in a way that gives me some fun and doesn't merely move the thingy from point A to point B?" Get creative! Find pull and tug-of-war opportunities that give you exercise while also hopefully creating some mayhem!

Among PD's "rope" toy ideas:

* Curtain sashes;

* Lamp and appliance cords;

* Belts, scarves, and bathrobe ties;

* Cell phone, computer, and smartphone cables;

* Garden hoses;

* The cat's tail (if you unfortunately share your pad with a feline)

See? Your very own version of *Toy Story*. Not live toys but a life of toys!

Voila! Home, sweet FAO Schwarz. Let your games begin!

RANDOM PD THOUGHT

IT'S MY TOY AND I'LL
CRY IF I WANT TO

When Lesley Gore sang that old "My Party" ditty, she was bawling over some guy named Johnny who stepped out on her with some chick named June.

I'd say "that's sad and all" but I'm sure you agree that our humans' romance up and downs are pretty silly and dull when compared to our deep love of . . . that certain toy.

And according to my research, the toy you are most drawn to, or possessive of, or slobbery with, or even sobbing over like Ms. Gore did over Johnny, depends on a bunch of factors.

If you are a retriever or hunter, for example, animalmedical. com says that toys can be "a substitute for prey" that you would otherwise be stalking, killing, or retrieving.

Some of us are drawn to chew toys because they quiet anxiety and help us chill out. And animalmedicalnc.com says that in the case of puppies, chewing can relieve the pain associated with teething. And get this: The site says that the reason a toy with our Mommy's or Daddy's scent on it is so calming is cuz it makes us feel like "a member of the pack" is with us.

Sometimes our toys are a substitute puppy for us. Iheartdogs.com says female dogs that get obsessed with a stuffed animal could be her maternal instincts shining through. The toy could remind her of a puppy, and she could feel an emotional connection to her surrogate baby. Animal Medical's site says even us boy dogs will exhibit the behavior from time-to-time, play-act mothering with their toys. The toy satisfies a deep instinct to nurture and protect.

To me, a squeaky toy is just a squeaky toy. Animal Medical says that for some of you, though, the squeak "sounds like the cry of prey after it has been nabbed by its predator." Apparently many of us are driven to find the source of the sound and will shred the toy in search of it and then eat the parts!

The best toy fact in my opinion, though, is the one that is obviously about Dog, my most favorite-ist toy on the whole Earth. It's this one from the iheartdogs site:

"Not every dog has a specific toy they love the most, but those that do become as attached to their toys as a toddler is to a favorite teddy bear. These one-toy pets cherish their chosen toys for months and years." So true! I am three and Dog is nearly my age! (Um, except I think two years ago, and then one year ago, Dog suddenly looked all fresh and new and I am scared the aliens cloned him! Or maybe Mommy went to Petco...)

Oh, and back to Ms. Gore and her sobbing. At least if Johnny was a toy the waterworks would make sense. Middogguide. com says the most common reason dogs cry when carrying toys is that they want to bury or hide the toy but they cannot find a place to bury or hide it, causing them to cry.

But it's their toy and they'll cry if they want to.

Chapter Four

A NEW MEANING TO "OFF THE LEASH"

TRAIN YOUR HUMAN LESSON #4: DEFYING DOG PARK DICTUMS

I love Poo.

Likely you do, too. But, I mean I loooooove Poo. No, I mean PD and Poo are a Thing, we are in love. Like Minnie and Mickey, like Lady and the Tramp, like Belle and the Beast, like Simba and Nala.

I would marry Poo if dogs could marry and if Poo would have me. I would write poetry about Poo. In fact, I have written poetry about poo. In "The Tao of Poo," Chapter Three of *Get Me Out of Here!*, I wrote the sublime "Ode to a PD Poopie." That Emerson-like work no doubt inspired awe and admiration of poo in the minds of our human readers who so ridiculously call it "a waste product."

Anyway, I mention all that to say this:

I really don't appreciate it that Mommy clamps right down on all my fun when *all* I am doing is trying to eat a bit of poopie when we are at the dog park.

There. I admitted it. Oh, c'mon! Don't look at me like you have a bit of throw-up in the back of your throat reading that or something. As if you haven't at minimum fantasized about it and at most taken a little taste. We are dogs. We like poo. Own it. And, er, if you can get away with it, *eat* it. Trust your Alpha Dog PD: it truly is nummy for the tummy.

Or at least I think it is. I mean, every stinking time we are at the dog park and I am racing about playing with my pals and happen to come across some nice reeky pile of poopie that a very thoughtful human "forgot" to collect, and as I enjoy sniff-sniff-sniffing that eau de poopie scent we all want bottled . . . well, I will just admit it. I start fantasying about my love for Poo and the next thing you know my salivating mouth is nearing my soul mate and then—

"PD! No! PD! Get away from there! Don't you even think of putting that in your mouth or we are leaving!"

Yep, the Warden. Marching right toward me, poopie bag in hand, causing every human and dog there—including you-know-who, my secret crush, fawn girl pug—to stare and either laugh or bark. So mortifying. Especially the barking since every dog there would try the same no-no if they could get away with it. And every one of you reading this knows it.

Which gets me to our next lesson.

TRAIN YOUR HUMAN LESSON #4: DEFYING DOG PARK DICTUMS

As I made very clear in *Get Me Out of Here!* outside is where it's at. And the dog park is a great outside spot! When the weather is nice Mommy often takes me to the super fun James Hunter Dog Park, which has a ginormous outdoor enclosed area for dogs to romp and ruckus. Humans mostly just stand around watching us frolic (Mommy does lots of embarrassing Mommy things, too, like taking pictures and videos of me and yipping to get my attention for a pose when I am trying to play already).

So no complaints on the outside part, or the frolic part, or the poopies that "forgetful" humans leave for me to sniff-sniff part, or even the part about it being second to my Bark and Boarding once-a-week daycare, where there are only a handful of human caregivers in the playroom with us, unlike a billion Mommies and Daddies hanging around the park edges. That's all fine.

But what is with all the rules, furry friends? I mean, we already are leash-less and running free, right? That's two common human rules we already are skirting. So it should be pretty easy to skirt them all. It's time we do away with every single silly nilly nonsensical rule on the dog park fence. And that's the goal of this lesson.

I live in Arlington County, Virginia, home of eight dog parks. They all are governed by a bunch of moronic laws. And I know that wherever your dog park is located—whether in Arlington or Argentina—it has a list of preposterous, illogical regulations, all of which likely were crafted and patented by the same lunatic.

Here are some of rules at my dog park:

"DOGS LESS THAN FOUR MONTHS OLD ARE NOT PERMITTED."

Oh, I seeeee. So during puppyhood, your most playful age of all, you get to stay home while the other house hounds go on a road trip to Funville. Happy boredom! See ya soon!

"FEMALE DOGS IN HEAT ARE NOT ALLOWED."

What? How are we studs supposed to decide which girlie to ask to Friday night walkie then?

"NO FOOD OR ALCOHOL IS ALLOWED WITHIN THE BOUNDARIES."

Okay, booze, I get; don't need Mommy all soused up on her froufrou pinot grigio and tripping face-first onto some left-on-the-ground poopie. But *no food?* That's like taking your child to Disney and denying them the Mickey Waffle or a trip to Goofy's Candy Company. I mean, we're at what for us is a magical place! And they're gonna starve us?

"DOGS MUST BE REMOVED AT THE FIRST SIGN OF AGGRESSION."

Now hold on there, Hoss. What constitutes "aggression" to these party-poopers?

Oh wait. Here is the explanation on the Oppressors' rules list:

"AN AGGRESSIVE DOG IS DEFINED AS A DOG THAT POSES A THREAT TO HUMANS OR OTHER ANIMALS."

Well, sure, being a smallish dog, I don't want some Kangal shepherd mauling me. I'm down with the no biting mandate. I mean, what are we, beasts in the wild? No! We are beasts in the city! We are civilized beasts, for golly sakes.

But let's ease up a tad on the "aggressive" definition thing. Po-tay-to, Po-tah-to, ya know. What Big Brother defines as "aggression" might be romper room play for us. See, a soft playful muzzle on the neck is not drooling rabid fangs on that same nape. Nor is frisky, boisterous dog wrestling the same as what's depicted in that *Off the Chain* pit-bull fighting documentary.

So if we are just aggressively playing or aggressively barking or, um, aggressively wee-weeing or something, then leave us be, right? I mean, we are out at the park having fun, for the love of dog.

"A HANDLER/GUARDIAN MAY BRING IN NO MORE THAN THREE DOGS AT A TIME."

Well, you solved that one by leaving the poor puppy at home.

"PROFESSIONAL DOG TRAINERS MAY NOT USE A DOG PARK TO CONDUCT BUSINESS."

Darn right. But after you dogs master all the lessons in this manual, you can bet that *human* trainers (us!) will be conducting plenty of business at dog parks and everywhere else!

"GUARDIANS/HANDLERS MUST ALWAYS REMAIN WITH THEIR DOG AND BE IN VIEW OF THEIR DOG."

Well, this is harebrained nuttiness. What, I'm racing around like greased lightning with slowpoke Mommy alongside? I'm flirting with my secret crush fawn girl pug and Mommy is chaperoning like she's June Cleaver? Or if not right up in my grille—when I'm "aggressively" playing—Mommy is staring me down from feet away like we are squaring off in a western saloon duel?

"GUARDIANS/HANDLERS, PRIOR TO LEAVING A DOG PARK, MUST FILL HOLES DUG BY THEIR DOG."

So if Picasso time-traveled here and made Mommy a purdy picture, she'd, what, paint over the canvas? Our holes are works of art, right? We dug a perfect hole! And then, poof! Filled!

"DOG GROOMING IS NOT ALLOWED IN ANY DOG PARK."

Thank Heaven! The only law that isn't a bunch of hornswoggle.

To pass this training lesson, you need to master:

NEW AND IMPROVED WORLDWIDE DOG PARK RULES, BY PD THE PUG

Old:

"Dogs less than four months old are not permitted."

New:

"Beginning at age two weeks, it's play time!" (I mean, at about the same age, a little fledgling basically gets bird Mommy's claw in his feathered fanny as she announces, "It's fly time! Don't let the nest hit your butt!" and boots him right out in the wild blue yonder. And that sounds scary, not fun like play time!)

Old:

"Female dogs in heat are not allowed."

New:

"Female dogs in heat have priority privileges." (Unlike discriminating humans, we invite females in heat, cold, lukewarm, or any other terms from Marco Polo swimming pool games.)

Old:

"No food or alcohol is allowed within the boundaries."

New:

"No boozed-up humans or their devil juice allowed. However, all foodstuffs other than those toxic to dogs are now available in our ten newly added large bins near the water bowls. " (Individual dog parks will have sign-up boards for humans to bring and sort food.)

Old:

"Dogs must be removed at the first sign of aggression. "

New:

"Dogs can't bite. Dogs can aggressively nibble, nudge, nuzzle, and annoy. Dogs can't bully. Dogs can aggressively gnaw bully Sticks, however. " (And what happens in Fight Club stays in Fight Club. "You do *not* talk about Fight Club!")

Old:

"A handler/guardian may bring in no more than three dogs at a time. "

New:

"A handler/guardian can bring up to, heck, 101 dalmatians or any other breed. " (It's a *dog* park. I don't see a limit on humans at the *human* park).

Old:

"Professional dog trainers may not use a dog park to conduct business. "

New:

*"Dogs who have achieved 'PD the Pug Human Trainer Certification'
may use a dog park to conduct human training business."* (Please
show your PD-paw-printed card at the entrance gate.)

Old:

*"Guardians/handlers must always remain with their dog and be in
view of their dog."*

New:

*"Guardians/handlers must always remain six feet from their
dog unless entering or exiting park, or when bringing a snack
to a tired dog from the treat bins (treat bin information above)."*
(PD note: Thank Heaven! About time dogs got to try out
this "six feet of space" thing we were always hearing about
during Covid.)

Old:

*"Guardians/handlers, prior to leaving a dog park, must fill holes
dug by their dog."*

New:

*"Guardians/handers, prior to leaving a dog park, should spend sev-
eral meditative moments touring the grounds and expressing admiration for all holes."* (PD note: Particularly investment-savvy
humans might consider their financial futures and snap pics
of their mastiff's Matisse-like masterpiece to sell online.)

Old:

"Dog grooming is not allowed in any dog park."

New:

"Dog grooming is not *allowed in any dog park!"* (Or even at the groomer's if we can help it!)

So there we go! As of this book's publication date, the New and Improved Worldwide Dog Park Rules by PD the Pug are officially mandated! Just think: The first set of rules you will enjoy heeding!

(Alpha Dog note: While I couldn't take Mommy through rules that did until now did not exist, I did start subtly training her in anticipation of coming changes. Stuff like digging in the park like I was digging to China; acting like a dog pied piper and luring many more than the three allowed dogs to follow us though the gate; barking like a rabid cur ("aggressively"); whining for the forbidden snacks that I happen to know she has in her pocket; and, just for giggles, working hard to undo any of her recent grooming attempts by getting splashed on near the pool and then dive-bombing straight into the dirt.)

RANDOM PD THOUGHT

I'D PEE ON DORIS RICHARD'S GRAVE (ER, FIRE HYDRANT)

Doris Richard is now one of my favorite humans.

This friend to dogs everywhere was instrumental in developing the first-ever dog park back in 1979!

According to Theparkcatalog.com, what's now Berkeley's Ohlone Dog Park is situated along a vacant strip of that remained after the construction of a BART subway station. It was supposed to be used for silly human residences.

But our Ms. Richard and her activist pals had other ideas! They took over the property and called it the "People's Park Annex."

Part the "People's Park" was used as an off-leash area where doggies could play. Ms. Richard "was instrumental in gathering petitions, working with the animal control workers and approaching city officials about officially designating the area for dogs."

The site says officials were skeptical at first, concerned about liability and insurance. So as a cautious first step the area was designated as an "experimental dog park."

And then—yippee!—in 1979, the first off-leash doggie playground in America became official! It was named Ohlone Dog Park. And then in 1983, according to Berkeleyplaque. org, the nonprofit Ohlone Dog Park Association was founded to help maintain it.

Dog friend Doris—the longest-standing association president—went to Heaven in 2009 but her legacy continues!

And we dogs all need to pay homage to this wonderful woman's memory by marking her memorial fire hydrant erected on the site in honor of her dedication and drive.

Berkeley road trip!

Chapter Five

YOU (PERFECTLY) DIRTY DAWG, YOU

TRAIN YOUR HUMAN LESSON #5: GOODBYE GROOMING

Last month, I had what will forever go down as one of the most horrific, terrifying and, okay, embarrassing moments of my young pug life.

I mean I'd heard of this torturous activity, but it seemed . . . I don't know, like something children would be told sitting around a campfire, or maybe by that Santa Man to make them be good! It was a ghost story, a fairytale, a rumor, a bogeyman.

I mean . . . *anal sac expression*? Haha, good one. Had me going there for a minute! Psych!

Well, no. Not so much. A few weeks ago, I did the dreaded scoot-scoot. Don't look at me like that. You've itched your butt across the floor a hundred times so don't pretend you are Nana or Toto and all perfect or something.

Look, long anxiety-inducing nightmare story short—and it's all a blur now: In the car, strapped to a table, latex gloves snapping on, a thumb and forefinger "gently" (?!) squeezing and then . . . basically I think I passed out at that point? I came to in the carrier in Mommy's car feeling like I escaped a prison hazing! Shell shock! Counseling! Medication! Well, at least a cuddle and my bully stick but better than nothing.

Uh oh. Hold on. Some of you don't look so good. Do you need a minute? Look, I'm sorry for conjuring up what you try to convince yourselves was merely a bad dream. But we need to dog up and deal. It happened, my pet pal. Your sacs were squeezed. That human shoved his hand there and did that to you. I'm so, so sorry. But let that disgusting, detestable, dreadful memory fuel your resolve to master your training lessons!

And since you already are lying there on Dr. PD, PhD's sofa— looking like some horror-struck war survivor—I'll just pass you the tissue box and let you cry it out, cry out every ghastly bit of grooming and every hellish health procedure. Let it go. Let it all go. Every time you dreamed of waterboarding after bath time; every time you awaited mockery at the dog park after having your fur shorn to near transparency; every time you wondered if that dental scrub was going leave you gumming your kibble; every time just knew you'd be deafened by that Q-tip...

Every time you thought, "For the love of Lassie, just let me channel my brothers and sisters in the wild and enjoy stink! Mange! Plague! Scoot-scoot! Let me be a *dog*, doggone it! I happen to like fecal matting in my fur!"

Look, I get it that a lot of you are crying now. But it's time to dog up! Untuck your tail and let me put a big drooly smile on your muzzle as you imagine your smelly, slovenly, scruffy, stinky, matted, mangy, mucky, uncombed, unkempt, *ungroomed* self after mastering our next lesson.

But First: Dog DNA and Our Fondness for the Foul

Before you follow along as I reprogram Mommy to never again have me bathed, nail-clipped, ear-Q-tipped, nasal fold-wiped, sac-probed, or go through any other atrocity at the groomers or home, Professor PD has a quick history lesson on why the love of all things stink is in our DNA.

According to Pedigree.com, the reason we dogs love to reek is instinctual, harkening back to days of yore when our wild ancestors would mask their scent to help them sneak up on their prey. The site gives the example of wolves that "have been observed rolling in animal carcasses or the droppings of plant-eating animals, to cover up their own smell during the hunt."

Mmmmmmmm . . . Oops! Sorry, zoned out there for a sec. But that sounds so Fun! I live in hoity toity Arlington, Virginia with hoity toity Mommy. I would give a lot to come across a carcass to roll around in! PD the Pug just covered in dead animal leakings and gloriously putrid juices.

And there's more to this love of stink thing. According to Vetstreet.com, dogs not only have millions more scent receptors than humans do, but we also are polar opposites from them when it comes to choosing scents that (according to their misguided understanding of what smells good) repel rather than attract (the site's words, not PD's). Mommy likes to sniff aromas the site calls "fresh, floral, and fragrant," while I relish a big whiff of—as the site puts it—"the dirty, dead, and disgusting, or the rank, rancid, and revolting."

Well. If Mommy wants to mask her scent, I can't talk good sense—or good scents—into her. But I'm done being Mr. Clean. And so are you. Eau de stink, au natural is in our futures. Ahhhhhhhhh. Natural!

TRAIN YOUR HUMAN LESSON #5: GOODBYE GROOMING

SCENARIO ONE: THE GROOMING DEPARTMENT

Look, this section is very hard to write. I am certain any shrink would say I have PTSD (Pug Traumatic Stress Disorder) from my many visits to the diabolical den that is Bark and Boarding's Grooming Department, just as you no doubt have recurring nightmares from your own visits to that den of iniquity at your own daycare or grooming place. I do love my Sunday Funday daycare at B&B but the demonic lair must be shut down or it'll be zero stars for B&B on Yelp from PD!

Anyway, as horror-stricken as I am just thinking of the grooming department, I knew that if we dogs are going to put an end to these ridiculously unnecessary grooming ordeals imposed on us by misguided humans once and for all, Coach PD had to take one for his team.

Yes, for you, for all of us, I headed into that satanic spa, and this time I decided to turn the tables on those ghouls! And thanks to me you soon will know exactly what to do next time your human drops you off for what is supposed to be a drowning or a deafening, er, I mean a bath or an ear cleaning. Or something else on your groomer's menu of misery.

Here is what happened during my hopefully last-ever trip to that wretched room. Pay attention! Follow your PD pack leader! And then forever stop smelling like a department store perfume counter after bath time or looking like a cue ball after a "fur trim."

Here we go, off to hell.

By the way, while Mommy does the minor league stuff like check my nasal fold and ears and swabs the yuckies, mostly she just looks me over to see what maintenance she deems needed to keep me the most handsome dog that ever graced Earth. And then she farms that out to the evil side of Bark and Boarding.

My usual—soon to be but a bad memory!—of the B&B Grooming Department grooming routine goes like this:

Monthly water torture, er, cleansing, in gigantic round vat while tethered to a rope to prevent drowning; monthly nail drilling down to the nubbies; weekly tooth scouring to nearly bloody gums. If I had a coat to cut, I might be shorn to within an inch of my life! There are other treacheries on their menu I could be "enjoying," and I am reminding myself while reminiscing that I need to thank my sweet Lord that so far I haven't needed more anal probes!

But no more. No more for me, no more for you. I know you will be so proud and also so envious to learn that because of my shenanigans at my last visit, I am the first-ever dog to be welcome with open arms to daycare but forever banned from the grooming department. Yippie! Banned! Forever! No more smelling like a Glade Plug-in!

My final trip to the underworld went thusly:

Mommy and I arrived at B&B for my bath, nail Dremel, and tooth scrub. The second my paws hit pavement I quickly jerked on the leash just enough to roll around the parking lot and get a bit of oil and other blechies on my already dirty coat.

Mommy left after handing me off to the smiley front desk person who then turned on me and forced me to walk the gauntlet to that chamber of horrors.

Just for giggles, I peed on the wall on the way.

As the grooming room door creaked open like in a scary movie, I calmed my racing heart by reminding myself that I was about to turn the (grooming) table on this tormenter. I was about to get free of fruity!

And after the mischief I made, they were pretty doggoned justified to expel Mommy and me from all future froufrou fuss at that place.

1. DEATH TO THE DREMEL

Tending to the talons was first on the list. But you know what? I like my Howard-Hughes-yellow-corkscrew nail fantasy and was proud of the month-long growth. I secretly love clicking around the house "helping" Mommy have an excuse to get the hardwood floors refurbished. And scratching loudly in my crate in the middle of the night when I feel like saying howdy. And scuffing up the walls when I'm bored. Clearly you can understand my reluctance to give them up.

So, as I was harnessed to the table and my furry foot was raised and the fur was pushed back to access my would-be claw, and the groomer neared with dreadful Dremel to begin the ear-splitting whirring and I was seconds away from being nearly nail-less . . . I went on offense!

First, I faked terror-eyed choking to get the harness removed. Once unrestrained, I was free to chew through the Dremel cord as well as send sanding bands, mandrels, safety glasses, and other nail-cutting necessities flying hither, thither, and yon.

Howard Hughes is dead; long live Howard Hughes!

2. "OH THE SHARK BITES..."

Next up was scrubbing the PD pearlies. This abomination actually is a weekly occurrence if you can believe it, so it was extra icky that Mommy did a trifecta nail/teeth/bath in one visit! Okay, it's just a toothbrush and some tasty pasty and not like the infrequent times the evil vet knocks me out to scale and scrub and polish enough to make me look like a Hollywood celebrity. But still! We dogs don't want some human sticking their paws in our maws and rubbing brushes or rubber-brush covered forefingers over our personal teeth! Stick your hand in your own mouth and just toss me a dental chew and let's call it a truly smiley day!

So, being so done with this demonic would-be dentist, PD staged another blitzkrieg! Just as the groomer neared with the brush, I dodged left, pounced on the newly opened new tube of tasty pasty with the full fourteen pounds of PD, and watched the minty goop squirt out and splotch the groomer's smock and gooey up his hair, as well as plop drops on the table and, annoyingly, on my coat.

Next, since I was already channeling Rex the Wonder Dog and Hong Kong Phooey and thus possessing superdog strength, I won a tug-of-war with the groomer, snatching the brush away and chewing it to unusable-ness and tossing it on the floor; I raced to the dental container to knock the remaining dental paraphernalia to the floor but was halted by the long arm of the law, er, groomer. We stared one another down like two cowboys in a saloon donning toothpaste instead of Stetsons on our heads.

3. BAN THE BATH!

I had to give it to the groomer—such stamina! Acting like my hijinks were nothing more than a moment of tomfoolery and that he had regained the upper hand . . . it was off to the worst of all rituals a poor dog can be put through. Yep, you're way ahead of me: It was the dreaded bath time. I know, I know. But hang in there. Master this and forever you will happily reek.

So, as the tether (noose!) was attached to allegedly prevent me from going under and I was lowered in the bubbly water-filled vat, I pulled the greatest of all my hijinks! I finally got sweet relief from holding my poopie in all day so that I could poopie in my bath! Genius, right? And as the water browned, the attendant jumped to attention and got PD the heck out of that bath-cum-sewer. And a big ol' body shake helped PD Picasso paint the room's walls in sepia tones. Then I tore up a bunch of rags and attempted to upend the vat (but at just fourteen pounds, well, even channeling Underdog at his most unstoppable, there was no way that bad boy was going over) just before I was captured, hosed down, and cocooned in a huge towel and carried to the wind tunnel, er, dryer.

The groomer did not look pleased as he blasted my little body with that warm wind. There was toothpaste on his smock and in his hair; he was stepping on Dremel bands and sporting flecks of PD poopie on his face and forearms. But it was a small price to pay for the call I knew a certain someone was about to receive. I knew Mommy would be, er, a tad disappointed but just think of the money I was about to save her on grooming!

When she arrived wearing the most shocked expression I've seen to date (which is saying something considering she has had the joy of my presence for three years now), I knew I had succeeded in my goal. I overheard only snippets of her conversation with the front desk human, but I caught "banned," "ejected," "expelled," "evicted," and other heart-warming words describing my new unwelcome status with the grooming department. Mommy gave me a brief stink eye before scooping up her not-quite-flower-smelling baby and doing quite the walk of shame out the door.

Hooray! Banished from the groomer! Mission accomplished, right? And you're now ready with a list of things to do at your own groomer, right? Well, hate to yank your leashes but whoa there, buddy. We have one more grooming lesson to learn.

SCENARIO TWO: GROOMING AT HOME

After being banned from the grooming department (so tragic . . . not!) and still being considered unkempt by misguided humans like flower-smell-worshipper Mommy, I was subjected to Plan B, aka grooming at home.

Fans of *Get Me Out of Here!* might remember Chapter 11, "Boo for Bath Time," which started off with my reminiscing about my first bath. It was the day after Mommy brought me home from my birth home, Howling Hills Kennel, at eight weeks. And that bath actually wasn't terrible. I was pretty tiny and Mommy bathed me in pot! In the sink! She gently washed my little body, delicately rubbing the soap into my fur and then she lovingly swathed me in a big fluffy towel, making sure I was all warm and snuggly as I got all dry.

So given that the most "grooming" I was dealing with as a baby was some gentle spa days in the sink, imagine my near-devastating distress when, a few months later, I was taken to the groomer for the first time and introduced to Dante's nine concentric circles of torment. Well, maybe not nine types of grooming, but a lot!

Anyway, now that we'd been (yessssss!) banned from the grooming department, it was up to Mommy to take over the PD preening regimen. And those of you dogs who actually are learning the new tricks I'm teaching you might be a step ahead and already congratulated your Alpha Dog for not letting that happen. Yep, things have not gone as she'd hoped.

Suffice to say:

- ❧ Baths are extinct and PD can stink;

- ❧ Nails are so long I am considering pedicures to show them off with even more pride;

- ❧ Ears . . . well, I can't hear quite as well, what with that bit of buildup in there, but that's what we want, folks: all the harder to hear their commands to sit, stay, and all the other nutty stuff we don't want to do;

❧ Teeth: While those little nips I "accidentally" kept giving Mommy's fingers and arms when she would try to do the finger brush thing with the vet-approved toothpaste worked to scare her off of that mouth invasion, she is a wise one! She immediately started giving me some dental chews that reduce tartar and keep the pearlies pretty pearly. But I fear my next visit to the vet won't be for a simple brushing but rather that procedure where they sedate PD to do a complete oral exam, and complete, thorough cleaning and tarter removal. (I will prepare an offensive for that and have a game plan ready for you soon! For now, think "be very, very difficult," whatever that means to you.)

❧ My (very private!) Anal Area: Thankfully I've only needed that one recent anal probe and so I will deal with it when and if I get caught doing a scoot-scoot. Hoping that was a one-and-done.

Here's what I did and what you will do if subjected to any home grooming grotesqueries:

❧ Bath: Splash water all over your human, walls, and floor (ceiling, too, if you're, like, a Marmaduke-dog size); grab an open soap bottle in your mouth and shake it like you're having a seizure; pretend to faint and then once you're underwater, pretend to be drowning before jumping up and licking your human's face with your soaked muzzle to show all's well; and once they somehow get you out of the bath and attempt to swath you, grab the towel and shred it into cleaning rags (so helpful of you since your human now has a lot cleaning to do).

✿ Nails: As soon as your human goes to lift your paw and apply the clippers or, worse, the Dremel, dance around like you're on hot coals. That will distract them long enough for you get your chompers on the evil instrument and shake your head around like mad and then hide it in your bed and sit on it and growl. Sadly, our humans are smart enough to know that waving a bowl of dinner is the sultry girl fawn pug (pick your own secret love) that will draw us off our rumps, so this guarding won't work long term. So when they try again, let them do one nail but bark louder than Charlie the Golden Retriever who, according to Barkblaster.com, holds the Guinness record for loudest-ever bark: 133 decibels!

✿ Ears: If your nails are done first, pulling a Charlie might be enough to keep these Q-tip-free zones. But I encourage you all to have a meet up with dogs like me who are near award-winning tail chasers. Barking wasn't quite enough to dissuade Mommy even after the nail debacle, so I spun around like a whirling dervish for ten minutes. If they can't catch you, they can't swab you. If you can't spin, run!

✿ Er, um, anal stuff: I don't encourage biting as that will get you at best a long time out in the crate or no dinner and at worst a send-off to one of those scary dog bootcamps for the type of reprogramming we are trying to do to them. No biting! When and if I ever am taken to undergo this nightmare again, I plan to do the dervish and then the Charlie and then try doing those Kegel exercises humans do to control urinary incontinence *(PD note: why on Earth would you ever want to control urine? I mark all over the place every chance I get!).*

🐾 Any other dog body care: Hopefully at this point, your human has read the memo and gets it that flower smell is finished. But if they try other grooming moves on you, channel Charlie, baby, channel Charlie!

You are now free to stink. Long live stink! You successfully went on the offensive and now you smell offensive. Good dog!

RANDOM PD THOUGHT

YOU'RE GETTING VERY SLEEEEEEEPY

Our humans seem to spend a lot of time—and likely some of our treat money—at the pharmacy getting pills and potions and pomades that allegedly help with everything from insomnia to heartburn to toenail fungus. Help for whatever ails you is on display at the CVS Cure Carnival.

And that's all well and good. Have at it, Mommy, go buy this week's exciting elixir for your calloused heel or today's must-have moisturizer for your split ends. And I'm sure you, too, live with humans who are forever trying the next magical bean to improve health woes real and imagined (Mommy has an entire drawerful of "wonders that weren't").

But we must draw the line at drugging the *dog*! And since we've been talking about the horrors of grooming, I thought this was the time to mention this in case your human thinks this is their Hail Mary to get you groomed. You are working hard on your grooming training lesson and the last thing you need is for your human to slip you a mickey!

Because that's exactly what is going on for many of you and your pals. They are *drugging us* before putting us in the car! It's true!

According to Bondvet.com, there are a couple levels of anxiety we dogs experience. The site says the lower level concerns stuff like visiting the vet or being adopted into a new home. Then there is the next level, the things that bring "short-term but intense anxiety." And specifically mentioned are travel, storms and . . . wait for it: grooming and toenail trims(!).

And if training and sedatives and thunder shirts don't do the trick, this site and lots of others mention vets giving us medicine for episodes of intense anxiety, everything from OTC Benadryl to tranquilizers! Next thing you know you are wasted and strapped down in Dr. Evil's barber chair or strapped to the Dremel table!

Oh. And by the way, Bondvet.com does mention twelve signs of anxiety in dogs. Gee, tell me if any of these happen to you at the groomer (*hint: all of them*):

- ❀ Attempts to escape
- ❀ Ears pulled back
- ❀ Crouching and making themselves as small as possible
- ❀ Tail tucked between legs
- ❀ "Whale eyes" (eyes open so wide you see the whites!)

🐾 Panting

🐾 Pacing

🐾 Trembling

🐾 Tense muscles

🐾 Bathroom accidents or anal gland release

🐾 Barking excessively

🐾 Sometimes growling, showing teeth!

Seriously? Sedation? Um, here's my idea: *no grooming.*

What's next? 'Shrooms and other hallucinogens and psychedelics? Be. Very. Afraid.

Chapter Six

(UN)HAPPY HALLOWEEN!

TRAIN YOUR HUMAN LESSON #6: DITCH THE DOG DUDS

There is a mortifying video of your pal PD—on Instagram and YouTube and Facebook and Lord knows where else in that Cloud thingy where even God is chuckling over it—wearing a Frankenstein suit.

And a Dracula suit. And a black bat suit. And a werewolf suit. And a skeleton suit.

This horrific embarrassment, which posted on Halloween, is set to the old song "Monster Mash" and starts off at the haunted mansion gate scene at the beginning of the "Thriller" video. From that frightening opener it goes to shot after shot after shot of PD the Freak. In a graveyard. In all those costumes. Sitting, running, spinning around (trying to get the werewolf pants off, as I recall), and otherwise looking the fool.

At least Mommy's happy; it has gotten a lot of what she calls "views" and "likes." Um, seems I should get a vote, folks. I don't *want* it viewed; and I don't *like* it.

Apparently *every* human skipped over the part of *Get Me Out of Here!* where I thought I made clear that since dogs were born dressed in fur, we don't need (or like or want) clothing.

But even my own Mommy, who was the first proud reader of her little PD's first writing, clearly saw this as a suggestion and not a law because, I am telling you, half the boxes from Amazon and Chewy contain PD costumes! Here are just some:

- 🐾 Halloween Freak (five get-ups!)

- 🐾 Cop and robber (no lie: Mommy had a video made with PD in cop suit chasing PD in robber suit, all set to that old time show *Keystone Kops.* I don't care to recall the number of likes, thank you.

- 🐾 Valentine's Lothario (tux, tails, bow tie, rose)

- 🐾 St. Patrick's Day complete get-up, including green tunic and top hat and *Duck Dynasty*–length red beard

- 🐾 Easter Bunny

- 🐾 Uncle Sam

- Greek god complete with head leaves and gold and white gilding on the garment

- Superman

- Batman

- Spiderman

- Captain America

- Einstein (one of us is and it's not the crazy costume chick)

- Pirate (yep, includes hook for paw)

- Horse with actual stuffed cowboy riding my back

- Chicken and waffles (you have to see it to get it. I had to pose outside Mommy's beloved Silver Diner)

- UPS Delivery Dog

- USPS mail carrier

- Bumble bee

- Doctor (I posed outside of a hospital and everything)

- Viking

- Thanksgiving turkey (this post includes a short clip of my getting it off! Happy moment!)

- Hanukkah dog with menorah on my head

- Too many Christmas costumes to list (her friends couldn't decide which was funnier: PD as snowman or

PD as gingerbread man or PD as Santa's elf or PD as a Rein Dog carrying Santa on my back.)

❧ Bowties, ears, bandannas, T-shirts, hoodies, and many other dog togs that I have managed to block from my memory (the only one I barely liked was the "regal prince" one, which I am wearing on the homepage of my site PDThePugProductions.com because, hey, PD equals royalty. But even that momentary mind connection with my Chinese royalty companion ancestors did little to alleviate the embarrassment.)

(PD note: I am very, very scared Mommy will try to mess with this manuscript and sneak in a link to my Instagram so I am telling you right now that it most certainly is not pd.the.pug.)

Does your human subject you to this mortification? I know I am far from alone in this because I see dogs trussed up on walkies all the time! And that's just the simple stuff like bandannas and T-shirts and hoodies and, Lord save me, booties.

Just peer over your human's shoulder one evening when they are monkey-braining out on Google looking for dog clothes and see the monstrosities that come up. When Mommy found "viking" (yes, smarties, in fact it does include the viking suit, helmet and horns, and bonus headpiece (weird antler-looking thingy?), she got all smiley and immediately hit that *buy* button.

And as I write—God save the queen (in her human queen costume)—Mommy is ordering a mustard suit for her PD to model when summer picnics begin. Gotta love Instagram. Leaving my fine rep in ruins.

Well it's time to channel Channing Tatum and Gypsy Rose Lee and start the strip show. Get out of those clothes, dawg! Let's get to our next lesson!

TRAIN YOUR HUMAN LESSON #6: DITCH THE DOG DUDS

One of Mommy's favorite iPhone videos is the one she shot of me when I was maybe four or five months old. I'm three now but she and her goofy friends still pull it up when they need a good guffaw at my humbled expense. In it, I am wearing a white Velcro-on cape/shirt thing with a huge gold rhinestone skull and crossbones on the back. And I am spinning in circles and dragging it and my tiny body is zigzagging across the floor, trying to get it off.

So my first memory of being in a costume is trying to get out of a costume. And nothing has changed since.

Well, that's no longer true, and thanks to my ingenuity in adding this training lesson to the curriculum it won't be true for you furry friends (who are supposed to wear fur and not clothes) either. It occurred to me that we can't possibly enjoy our new lives of ease while dressed as Mister Potato Head or Xena the Warrior Princess. I mean, what? You're going to dominate the dog park in your flying pig suit (yep, fellow canines, get your own from Target)? Well, no. No, you're not. The only costume you'll ever model again is this year's canine. No more feeling (or dressing) like a circus clown!

(PD note: Thankfully Mommy fears snakes and clowns. No clown suits [yet] on PD.)

So let's get naked, baby.

Now, while PD's costume closet doesn't exactly rival Mommy's Carrie-from-*Sex-in-the-City* wannabe armoire, I have a lot of clothes! And since it's early on in Mommy's total reprogramming, I do have a lot left to chew holes through or otherwise destroy, but thanks to what I am about to teach you, that number certainly is dwindling. I have a way to go, but one taco costume (yep, see Instagram) at a time.

Anyway, this whole-clear-the-closet chore required a lot of experimentation. It's one thing to shake an Einstein white wig off your head and quite another to figure out the Velcro on the belly part of the sheepskin parka. So use my hard work to make your naked days come more quickly.

DO DO THE FOLLOWING:

🐾 The canine's canines are your best friend here. I found chewing holes in outfits when Mommy was turned away was an effective way to make my outfit look less Ghostbusters crew member and more Charlie Brown ghost costume in *It's the Great Pumpkin, Charlie Brown*. So gnaw away whenever your human's back is turned. Well, unless your human has you dressed in real viking chainmail, in which case you you'd chip your molar.

If your human insists on making you wear the costumes you filled with holes because—to quote one human who will remain anonymous—"I paid Chewy good money for that Washington Nationals dog jersey and mini hockey stick, and by golly, PD, you are wearing it and that's final!"—then you have to pretend you are at a costume ball and dance the night away. Dance and spin around like there are ants in your dog policeman pants and see if that helps shake loose the offensive garment.

❧ Be aware that some clothes might be more dog-form-fitting than others and can't easily be grabbed by your teeth—I'm talking to you, "Drinks well with others" T-shirt—so upping the dance game and playing whirling dervish or getting a few faux attacks of the zoomies might loosen the tighter togs a bit, depending on fabric type. It helped me rid my head of all hats and ears adornments as well as bring a little give to my rock star with guitar get-up.

(PD note: Despite your frustration with snugger stuff you can't get a tooth grip on, do not diet in an effort to loosen things that way. Because a) it would take months [if you were a pug, you'd never succeed] and b) we are not humans and do not diet unless forced to eat some barfy diet formula dog food! The goal of this whole PD Human Trainer Certification process is to be a happy hound, ruling the roost and all environs and eating until you burst like that Oompa Loompa kid. So no dieting!)

(PD note addendum: If you even entertained the idea of dieting to get out of your costumes, just put your tail between your hind legs and realize you sadly are not cut out for this program. Sorry to lose you, but I can't have a dieting-by-choice dog among those in the

Certification Club and possibly sharing that bad idea with other human trainer hopefuls.)

Whenever your human approaches with that day's costumery, pretend to be a vampire bat-attired bat out of hell and race around the house like your jowls are on fire. This got me out of a couple of outfits but only temporarily and mostly because princess "I also need to eat and work, PD!" got frustrated and had to give up for the day. But it's not a long-term solution and won't rid your wardrobe of that piece. But hey, a one-day victory sure beats a Christmas-tree-with-topper day. Even if only for twenty-four hours.

DON'T DO ANY OF THESE:

🐾 Waste precious time overly studying the inner mechanics of Velcro and zippers and (Lord!) buttons on shoes. Just stick to gnawing, dancing, spinning, and other active activities. Don't sit around poring over seamstress manuals, for dog's sake.

🐾 Make it simple for your human to dress you. Play dead dog. Let all limbs go completely slack. Become dead weight. Offer zero help as your human tries to strap a sailor hat to your head or tie on cowboy chaps or tie a magician's cape around your neck.

(PD note: Should your human start succeeding in the beginning stages of getting attire on any part of you, suddenly become Frankenstein's monster and come to life! "It's aliiiiiiiive!" Then

wiggle, waggle, hopscotch, and otherwise fight to prevent becoming fully clad.)

- ❧ Howl. While there are some anxiety-related reasons dogs do this type of communication, there are happy reasons too. According to Pethelpful.com, some dogs howl when they achieve something or feel excited. The site says hunting dogs, for example, usually howl when they detect game or succeed in a hunt. And the last thing we need is for our human to start thinking we are yelling, "Success! Hooray! It's costume time!" like some overzealous overachiever human raising a fist whenever they see a costume or a Chewy box we fear includes same.

- ❧ Diet (covered above)

This lesson will take much perseverance. It's certainly not a one-and-done. You will shed your clothes the faster you shred (and dance and play dead). But it will take time. Some of you are blessed with a human who only subjects you to a florescent orange bandanna or an I-heart-snacks (yep, own it!) T-shirt or the annually donned pair of bunny ears. Others (like Alpha PD) have a human who seems to shop online for your wardrobe as often as they do their own. You have a bigger closet-purging job ahead. But you will succeed! You will reach naked nirvana!

No more Queen Elizabeth collar ruff! *No more* embarrassing clothes!

Welcome to the PD nudist camp. Where even towels are banned.

RANDOM PD THOUGHT

IS IT "BUTT" NAKED
OR "BUCK" NAKED?

I saw a piece on Bark.post.com that backs up not only the normal-ness of our nakedness but also just maybe backs up my personal thought that humans should go naked too!

The site reports on a study conducted by the psychology department at Massey University in New Zealand that sought to answer whether we dogs were affected by the clothes people wear, and specifically whether patterns affected us.

The idea behind the project was that color-specific warning systems are instinctive and coded into our genes. Whether or not we ever have experienced a negative outcome associated with a specific color pattern—as seen on, say, poisonous snakes or even poisonous caterpillars—we instinctively avoid that pattern.

Well, sure we do that in the wild, but this research shows that maybe we do it in very urban Arlington, Virginia, and wherever you and your human live!

The researchers observed twenty-two shelter dogs "as a stranger approached each of their kennels wearing a long-sleeved shirt with different patterns, including narrow black and white stripes, horizontal and vertical stripes, unequally spaced stripes, and no stripes at all."

Results? Clothing = traumatized dog!

Okay, no, but it does say that "it turns out that the shirt the participant wore did impact the dog's behavior. The dogs were most active when they saw the shirt with the narrow, evenly spaced striped pattern and least active when they saw the solid-colored shirt."

And wait, here it is! Active was defined as submissive! "The behavior suggested that they were spooked by the shirts and felt uncomfortable or anxious around them. Pretty much how they would act if they encountered an animal with this pattern in the wild."

Yeah, pretty much. How 'bout Mommy and rest of you stop spooking us with your clothing?!

Naked is the new dressed.

Chapter Seven

FENG SHUI THE DOG WAY

TRAIN YOUR HUMAN LESSON #7: HARMONIZING *OUR* HOME

Mommy always goes all goo-goo over the pictures in those human home magazines. I can tell we are a click away from getting yet another useless adornment by her glaze-eyed stare as she fantasizes about the featured froufrou fringy pillows and bejeweled wall frames and other gilded garniture. I know that look, the mesmerized gaze of a woman imagining herself in a palatial estate rivaling Versailles in both its splendor and furnishings.

Ah, the furnishings. What is with our humans and the (wasted) time and (wasted) effort they put into making the house some resplendent Eden worthy of a cover feature in *House Beautiful?*

I get chairs. I get appliances (I'm cool with anything that leads to me getting food, so I agree that many types of appliances—refrigerator, toaster, stove, oven, even dishwasher for PD's dog dish—are crucial). I get cabinets (food!). I get tables too since humans need to sit somewhere to enjoy food.

But the stuff! All the stuff! Pillows, vases, sculptures, sconces! Sconces? I thought that was a hard sweet biscuity thing that Mommy gives me a taste of occasionally but *no*, it's a fancy-pants light decoration for the wall (why are lights on walls when we already have a bazillion lamps on a bazillion tables and also have two floor lamps?) and I know this because Mommy has five of them! Five sconces!

And more stuff! Rugs, mirrors, magazine holders, decorative trays, candles! So many candles! And candle trays! A tray for a candle, for the love of dog!

And Heaven help me, plants. And faux plants, too. Mommy has a really tall fake tree in her bedroom. A tree in a bedroom. We have a gorgeous Japanese maple out back that is way prettier, and plus, I'm allowed to pee on it, but I get "time out time" if I dare lift my hind leg around Mr. Fakey Face.

I could go on. But you get it. You likely are trying to focus on this manual whilst your human's grandfather and cuckoo clocks loudly chime or the Roomba sweeps around you or another Crate and Barrel box thuds as it's delivered to the door. So I'm sure I'm preaching to that YouTube-featured dog choir.

But it's not just the ridiculousness of it, the clutter of it, the money-that-should-have-gone-to-treats of it. It's that it's affecting my peace of mind. My Zen. My chi. My tranquility. My om. And yours as well.

You already have mastered—or are leaning how to master—the food allocation and grocery and treat lists, the walkies, the outings. You've done away with grooming. You have shredded your costumes. You have so many toys the elves can't keep up with production. But one big thing remains: The final step to achieving true peace.

What you need is a more dog-friendly home. Like mine is now that I harmonized it the PD way as I came up with this very important and final training lesson.

To reach pure Zen you need a pure dog den, you need a home like mine is getting to be, one that says "the place has gone to the dogs, er, rather, a dog. And that's you, Mister or Missus New Master of the Realm. Yep, it is time to redesign your abode to better fit your new life with your now-trained human. So channel your inner Joanna Gaines and let's start demolishing walls, so to speak. Let's feng shui the dog way!

TRAIN YOUR HUMAN LESSON #7: HARMONIZING *OUR* HOME

So just what is feng shui and how can we use this concept to recreate our environs to help us better access the things we care most about?

Those of you who read *Get Me Out of Here!* know a bit about my and other pugs' connection to China. In long ago times, pugs were bred to be companions to Chinese royalty. As Wikipedia tells us: "The pet pugs were highly valued by Chinese emperors, and the royal dogs were kept in luxury and guarded by soldiers."

Feng Shui must be pretty great because it comes from China like the pugs of yore! Wikipedia calls it "an ancient Chinese traditional practice which claims to use energy forces to harmonize individuals with their surrounding environment."

Well, once I realized how very out of harmony we dogs are in a home environment that prioritizes sconces over doggie scones, I decided that the ancient Chinese practice could be "tweaked," if you will, to make our homes into real live dog houses: the type of house you would design for yourself if given the chance. And with this final lesson, that chance has arrived.

Again, in feng shui (the dog way or any way), the goal is harmony. And for us dogs to feel harmony, we need to have easy accessibility to food and toys and beds, right? So when I developed this lesson, I knew I had to train Mommy to make sure that the vast majority of items in the home and the majority of routes through the home are bought or designed with PD in mind.

Things that made the PD list (feel free to tweak as your own inner Buddha desires):

🐾 Any and all non-toxic-to-dogs food

🐾 Fat stuffy beds: one per room

- Toy boxes: one per room of our townhome (minimum ten toys per toy box)

- Treat cabinet with dog-accessible dispenser button for sudden cravings between meals

- All food-related human appliances

- All food-related human cooking and/or food prep implements

- Swing door built into front and back doors so I can take myself on a walkie by myself without Mommy if I feel like it

- Examples of things *not* on the PD list due either to their affecting an easy path to food-related places/items or my fat stuffy beds or my toy boxes and/or floor space for fun and frolic or to the new outdoor-access swing doors (these items are in the process of being removed and are now off the Mommy shopping list and are never to be reintroduced to the domicile):

- Floor Clutter:

- Floor vases/urns

- Floor plants

- Clothing strewn about instead of taken to laundry room by lazy, tired Mommy

- Magazine racks

* Ornamental tables that hold stupid stuff (one of Mommy's features only a fancy old bowl that was her grandmother Meme's and holds only potpourri?)

* Money-Wasting Decor:

* Wall sconces (bakery scones, however, are welcome)

* Expensively framed plaques with goofy pithy sayings

* Torchieres

* Greek-themed busts (Mommy has, erm, Apollo?)

* (Faux!) Ancient plates mounted on shelves (Mommy also has a big stone plate with the Fates. Well, their *fate* is the trash can!)

* Ornamental lighting in rooms with ceiling lights already there!

* Decorative pillows

* Collectibles

* Candles and candle holders

* Your own list might include:

* Deafening grandfather and other fancy-pants clocks (they get keep the one on the microwave because we need a timer for food prep)

* Fireplace log holders (store them in the garage!)

* Useless side tables

* Baskets

🐾 Chairs in "formal" rooms that are covered in plastic and never sat on (?)

🐾 Glass figurines and other sculptures

🐾 Dried pampas grass and other weeds human think should be displayed

And so much more you quickly will notice as you get into this lesson!

So now that you have your list, do what I am doing. If Mommy buys a money-waster or floor clutterer or anything not on the PD-approved list, I do one of three things:

🐾 Break it.

🐾 Eat it.

🐾 Shred it.

(Or otherwise make it go bye-bye.)

And my plan is working! Er, I mean, it's early, yet Princess Amazon orders and replaces things that "mysteriously" disappear or which "accidentally" are knocked over, peed on, chewed up, or otherwise ruined by PD faster than my little self can destroy them.

And, okay, I don't yet have a bed in every room; or ten over-stuffed toy boxes; or the built-in swing doors for outside access 24/7; or the paw-push dispenser button on the treat cabinet, but again, early days! And I'm doing stuff daily toward the goal, like dragging my beds (I do already have three so we are getting there) from room to room to show Mommy I want to nap everywhere and choosing a different room daily to play with my toys in and scratching the treat cabinet door like mad in an effort to create a hole. Stuff like that.

So far I have gotten permission to play all over the joint but no new toy boxes and a stink eye when my bed is found just beyond the left-open shower door. I pretend I need to pee when I don't so she will finally get tired of taking me out and decide to install those swing doors. And I do a faux faint after dramatically sniffing the air when she is slicing toxic-to-dogs onions in the hopes that one day soon she will be panicked enough to discard all deadly-to-dogs human food. So far I'm just playing Scarlett O'Pug and "fainting" a lot.

Of all our lessons, this final one likely will be the last to be realized as you have more renovation work to do than Tim "The Toolman" Taylor on *Home Improvement.* But you and I are in this for the long walkie and not just some quick backyard poopie, right? If you want to own the house and stop feeling like you're renting space in a home designed—planned! intentionally!—to slow your access to all the things you want while also offering poisonous provisions and screeching clocks and ugly pampas plants to gaze at and what-have-you.

For this lesson, you get a check mark if you achieve all that I have achieved in the PD Palace (soon-to-be, as of this writing) and if you are totally committed to transforming your own home to *your own home.*

Yes, it's a lot of work to redesign a house, Martha StewDog.

But once you clear that clutter and rewrite your humans' shopping lists and can those candles and their space-wasting ilk, you have the remainder of your happy days to eat, sleep, potty, and play how you want in your dog house.

Mirror my new attitude: The human can live here but "my house, my rules." And you and I will know we've succeeded in our remodel when our humans start saying the house is "going to the dogs."

Well, duh. Whole point, people.

And now . . . Marine Corps–worthy drum roll . . . Please rise from whichever of your several fat stuffy beds you are cuddled up in and wag that perked-up tail with pride as you finish this last of your lessons and spin in circles as I tell you: you now are (or soon will be) a PD-Certified (trademark) Human Trainer. Not only have you trained your human in all areas of dog life, but you also now have the opportunity to be an accredited teacher of other dogs and help PD in my effort to change our dog world to a perfect planet, one human at a time. (Contact PD for rates and regulations! Join today!)

You've done it! You've mastered these lessons and soon will master the master. You not only will rule your castle and the environs beyond, but you also will have achieved true serenity, peace, Zen, and tranquility. Imagine having this feeling as you rise and do your downward dog stretch every new morning and greet the day.

A clear path, free of human clutter. And a clear mind, clear of human clutter. Clear of both physical and mental messes. You own your house, your walkies, your dog park, your (now non-existent) grooming schedule, the timing and amount of food and treats, and your costume-free self.

(Looking good! Smelling great! Fattening up! From dog's life to a life of Riley. King and queen of the canine castle. Nice work, top dog. Nice work.)

PD the Pug
Training
Academy

Human Trainer
CERTIFICATE
by
PD the PUG

YOU DID IT!

You did it!

You now have passed each of our seven official lessons and thus meet our strict requirements and are qualified to become a *PD Certified Human Trainer.* Please fill out the registration form coming in the mail, and as soon as you receive your *PD Certified Human Trainer Diploma*[‡] in the post (please allow six to eight weeks for arrival), you are *PD Certified* and authorized to do the following:

Continue the reprogramming of your hapless human, fine-tuning any of the seven areas you believe require more effort and focus.

Train any other dog to earn their own *PD Certified Human Trainer Diploma.* Attend an annual refresher course in which you provide proof that your human remains well-trained and that the seven areas of the *PD Certified Human Trainer Program* remain under your control. During this class—taught by Alpha PD—you will learn of improvements in human training, as well as how to perfect areas in which you are lacking the complete upper paw.

[‡] Postage costs are charged to recipient

This course is not mandatory and carries a one-new-toy fee.

Three years of refresher courses entitle you to lifetime membership in the *PD Certified Human Trainer Association.* Association benefits include:

🐾 One annual walkie with Alpha PD

🐾 One toy donated from one of Alpha PD's multiple toy boxes

🐾 Your choice of half-gnawed Alpha PD bully stick or four treats from an open Alpha PD treat bag

🐾 One sniff of Alpha PD during annual walkie

🐾 One Alpha PD play date at day and time arranged by PD the Pug Productions.

(Final Alpha PD note: While you are free to lead your human through the lessons in any order desired, your Alpha PD suggests going in the order listed. It is especially important to begin with the food *chapter because if you are not in charge of the* food, *you are a hang dog, regardless of dominance in all other areas.)*

EPILOGUE

Oh no.

No no no no no no *no.*

What has PD done?

Mommy is in a ball on the floor kind of like a kitten. But like a human kitten. Like a human kitten who is mewling and mewling like their milk was all lapped up and they are so, so sad.

And I keep lick-lick-licking her face but it's not helping. It's only making her already wet-with-tears face wetter.

She's softly weeping and staring into space and looking like Nordstrom just declared bankruptcy.

Um . . . due to PD. All due to PD. This is all my fault.

If only I'd known! If only I'd seen the consequences of my actions. But we dogs aren't so good at looking ahead. Our focus generally is on the next treat or meal or the next walkie or the next poopie. I didn't know! I meant well! I thought my changes at home and beyond would be good changes!

And they were. They all were. For PD.

It has been a couple of months now since I began my jour-ney to complete doggie tranquility and wrote this manual to help you set off on your own path to both peace and power.

But if your mommy's or daddy's face looks anything like mine—and I am sadly assuming that is the case—you have no peace and aren't feeling that powerful either.

I know. I sure held the "power." Prince of PD Palace. Lord of the (former) Mommy Manor. Not to mention Dominator of the Dog Park, Overseer of the Toy Fiefdom, Warrior of the Walkie, Governor of My Grooming, Ringleader of the Refrigerator. And naked as the day—even in a snowstorm—now that costumes and coats are in tatters.

I'm sure your life either mirrors or—as you complete your lessons—will soon mirror mine. And it's a shattered mirror. In shards. Scratching up my little PD heart. And as I gaze upon my sweet sobbing Mommy, I realize that a broken mir-ror's seven years of bad luck would be a whole lot better than just the seven minutes of pain I've felt so far today.

Why didn't my googly eyes see this coming?

I mean, I know I've been pretty—okay, solely—caught up in my own wants and needs. I know I might have ignored a couple of warning signs, a handful of hints, a whisper in my soul that something wasn't quite right.

Okay, nothing was right! But I didn't know! I was just happy! And fat! And naked! And not accountable to Mommy or anyone or anything!

Seemed like such a great plan. I was certain that I—*me!* Alpha PD! A mild-mannered little black pug in Arlington, Virginia!—had developed the true and only path to true Zen for all dogs. Nirvana. I had arrived. And many of you had arrived or are just a lesson or two away from arriving on your own mountaintop.

But now Mommy is on her side on the kitchen floor, half in shock, half in hysterics, and I've fallen from the highest heights to the lowest valley. This catastrophe I caused now demands my comeuppance.

Where did it all go so wrong? All the food is mine, I rule the walks. I own the dog park. I'm drunk on toys. I'm free of bowties and—even in the dead of Washington winters—fleecy jackets.

And Howard Hughes would envy the nails that have grown so long they are curling under my paws and hampering my walk. Never mind my teeth that feel like they haven't seen a toothbrush since I was actually teething.

(PD note: I don't know if I'm stinky and likely neither do you because we dogs do really, really, really love stinky.)

But gazing upon Mommy and feeling her ache as she cries and cries, Alpha PD is forced to revisit a few (tons of, gobs of, mountains of) things I might possibly have glossed over while researching to write this training manual. Things that didn't fit Alpha PD's—or your—imagined perfect life and which thus were ignored.

And which refuse to be ignored any longer. For me—and I am sure for you—reality has come calling. For me, my precious meltdown has made clear to me that I have taken things too far. Like Arlington-to-Australia too far.

Everything is a mess. Mommy's a mess because I made a mess of the house, her schedule, her shopping lists, our walkies, our dog park trips, our (non-existent) visits to the groomer, her budget (I should open my own Toys 'R' PD company and be a spokesdog for Petco, PetSmart, Loyal Companion—every dog place selling treats and playthings).

Her *home.* Shambles. So many of her things removed, replaced, or outright destroyed as I sought to achieve my perfect PD-approved maze from bed to toy box to refrigerator to back door, a path unhampered by "human things," like clocks, and plants, and decorative tables and even those sconce things and other PD-rated eyesores.

But the only eyesore now is me. PD. I am the eyesore. I am the problem. I made Mommy fall apart. Because I decided that my "perfect" home and my happy walks and my allocation of food and treats and my wearing of a warm jacket in the snow and my already-stuffed-to-the-top toy box and even how many of Great Auntie Sheila's treats I could have now versus even a little bit later: that all of that was no good. That it had to be changed for the better.

For my better. For your better. But certainly not for Mommy's better. Or your human's better. And I know you are tucking your tail in in sadness too, as you contemplate the state of (messy) affairs in your own "perfect" dog home.

But is everything truly better? Is even one thing better over-all? If we are being selfish, maybe we stubbornly say yes. But if we are honest...

Our human's rehabilitation has gone too far. It's one thing to howl over actual abuse and another to gripe about imagined indignities or just not lording over the manor unrestrained, with no rules, no limitations, no boss but dog dog dog.

Well, it's time for us to clean up our act, literally and figura-tively. And to help you and me do that, I need to share some research I, um, didn't let get into my stubborn Alpha PD head when I was putting our training manual together. It didn't seem accurate . . . or, okay, convenient . . . at the time.

FOOD:

Golly, I am jolly. Like Santa jiggly jolly. I passed pleasingly plump miles ago. I'd be merely rotund *if* I went on a diet. Fat, fat, fat. And happy, happy, happy. Happier than I ever imagined I could be—running the refrigerator, captaining the cabinets, lording over the lists for the grocer and the pet store treat aisle. Saving none of our guest's PD goodies for "later." And munching every morsel found on the ground outside. Hooray for Porky PD.

FOOD REALITY:

Er . . . fat might not be where it's at. Not for any dog and certainly not for potentially obese breeds like pugs. Like me. But I'm guessing I'm not the only one (ahem) who needs to heed this warning from Vcahospitals.com: "Excess fat negatively impacts a dog's health and longevity. Obese dogs develop an increased risk for: many types of cancer, diabetes mellitus, heart disease, and hypertension. osteoarthritis and a faster degeneration of affected joints."

It also occurs to me that . . . while it is understandable to want to rid the fridge of toxic-to-dogs chow, it's not fair to not let Mommy have onions or raisins or macadamia nuts or—*Lord* help me—alcohol or chocolate. She likes (loves?) these and other PD no-no foods. She is sad without them. And since I've made it three years without her accidentally poisoning me, maybe I can trust her to keep the streak going.

So I'm reluctantly giving Mommy back the kitchen. And yes, the grocer and pet store pad.

And okay, I'm also giving her back charge over the allocation of guests' treats. I do want all of Great Auntie Sheila's cookies right this minute but since apparently there is a connection between too many cookies and lethargy and also a sore tummy, I have to be "reasonable." Mommy blathers on about "blah blah blah" pugs are an obese breed and so too many cookies can mean not only fat (yay fat!) but also diseases (boo diseases!). Hard one because I want all the cookies. But I don't want the sickies.

And mostly I'll try not to be so curious about stuff on the ground outside. Turns out the orange yarn story I mentioned in *Get Me Out of Here!* wasn't as cute a story as I thought. Mommy was super-duper scared when I kept vomiting and vomiting. It was late at night, and she had me scooped up to go all the way to Doggie General, but as I mentioned in Training Lesson #1, the doctor said to monitor me overnight and I turned out fine. But I guess my theory that "if it's PD eye level it can go in my tum tum" isn't quite accurate.

I hate when Mommy is right. But about all the food stuff . . . Mommy is right.

WALKIES:

My roams around the neighborhood and beyond are so carefree! Breeze in my flat face, dragging Mommy by my leash from bush to tree to hydrant and back again as I sniff and mark and poopie to my heart's content. In slow-mo. Or sometimes fast-mo. Mo mo me! Deciding on detours, captaining my course, ruling my route!

WALKIES REALITY:

Hmmm. Is it maybe, er, possible that PD needs a walkies co-pilot? I didn't love finding this: Dogs in charge of the walkie "lead to many behavioral issues that some regard as a 'breed trait' or 'personality,' when actually it is your dog being in charge of its humans. When a dog walks in front, it does not drain its mental energy. The dog is not relaxed, as it has the big responsibility of leading the pack. This mental anguish can build up inside of a dog" (dogbreedinfo.com).

DOG PARK:

I have always loved going to James Hunter Dog Park. Lots of fun friends—except that one un-neutered dog from *Get Me Out of Here!* who tried to mount me like twenty times when I was about six months old and left me traumatized. But every other dog is my good pal—to frolic and race around with. And since developing the new Dog Park Rules things have seemed even ten times better! I know that you too are loving ignoring all past ordinances as you invite all the friends you want, including puppies, flirting with now-allowed female dogs in heat, enjoying the now-permitted treats in the new yum bins, doing every type of frolic short of biting or bully-ing, and just having the time of your life.

DOG PARK REALITY:

As I write this it occurs to me that one of many reasons lead-ing to Mommy's inevitable nervous breakdown must have been the summons she got recently from Arlington County Circuit Court. My name wasn't on it since they don't know PD by name, but it was pretty clear who they were referring to when they sent her a notice saying, among other things:

"Violations of the (dog park) leash law, pooper-scooper law and running-at-large law can result in a summons to appear in court and a fine of $100...

"Guardians/handlers are legally responsible for their dog and any injury caused by them...

"Guardians/handlers must always remain with their dog and be in view of their dog...

"Guardians/handlers must always be in possession of their dog's leash...

"It is unlawful for any person who owns, possesses, or harbors a dog to permit that dog to create a frequent or continued noise disturbance..."

So it's one thing for us to have free rein and maybe quite another for our humans to lose their very freedom. Or even $100. Which Mommy now can barely scrounge up thanks to all her money going to toys, treats, and dog beds.

GROOMING:

In before-Alpha-PD-ruling-the-home-and-surroundings days, Mommy knew it was time for a monthly-ish good ol' Dremeling of the nails when she could hear the *click-click-click* of my nails as I walked around the hardwood flooring on the main level of our home.

Now, my nails are so long (I gave you the Howard Hughes vision earlier) that shortly before her breakdown, Mommy was on the phone with John at the flooring company to get a price for refurbishing the more-scratched-up-than-not wood. Of course, I would ruin the new floor too, but I guess her hope was that I'd either tire of ingrowns and hobbling or the beautified floors would remain new-looking a long while before the scratches showed through.

Anyway, I do love no grooming. You know as well as I do that a love of stinky and unkempt are in the genes. I mean, can you imagine our wolf ancestors getting manicures and blowouts? *No.* No, you can't. And think of the money our humans are saving each month not shelling out for doggie baths, teeth cleanings, nail trims, and other dog salon offerings.

(PD note: Um. Okay, I guess my other budgets—beds, treats, toys— are a wee bit up. But still.)

So I have to say—and I know you echo my opinion—smelly equals smug! Claws equal clout! Tartared teeth equal tough! Wax-clogged ears equals winner! In fact this is just a win-win-win-win (and win in any and all other grooming category to which our human used to subject us)!

GROOMING REALITY:

Um, okay, maybe I am not the champion I imagined I was in the grooming (or non-grooming) department. I was unhappy to read this: "Grooming a dog's nails, teeth, and ears may seem frivolous, but they're as important to your dog's good health as heartworm preventative and pest protection. Keep your dog healthy by performing these tasks every week" (dummies.com).

Get a load of this depressing news regarding teeth: "Brushing your dog's teeth regularly removes tartar and plaque. Although tartar starts in the mouth, if not removed it can then transplant to other parts of the body where it can build up and cause blockages that affect other organs and joints. Brushing regularly can also prevent heart disease, arthritis, and multiple other complications...

"Toxins from periodontal and other oral diseases are absorbed into your dog's bloodstream, and can damage the heart, kidneys, and liver which filter the blood" (1800petmeds.com).

And this on nails: "Long nails can turn a sound paw into a splayed foot and reduce traction, and they can cause deformed feet and injure the tendons over an extended period" (akc.org).

"Dogs don't walk correctly when the nails are too long and this strains the leg muscles and torques the spine" (abck-9fun.com).

And they can't even stay out of our ears!

"(Unless properly taken care of) the ear will trap dirt, debris, and moisture against the head with no airflow to reduce the buildup of harmful bacteria" (Merryfield.edu).

Oh. No. Please. Don't make us go back to baths! I am begging you! And at first the news appeared to be on our side. But, alas . . . no.

"In general, healthy dogs only need to be bathed if they smell. There's no reason particularly to bath a healthy dog, unless they're dirty" (abc.net.edu).

If you're like me, at first you thought that was great news, because to us we don't smell and we aren't dirty; we are *dogs* and we think smelly and dirty are good. But *no* this is written for humans! So, well, crud.

Aha! Finally a little good news. Apparently there is a limit on the frequency.

"But bathing too often can be detrimental to your pet as well. It can irritate the skin, damage hair follicles, and increase the risk of bacterial or fungal infections" (petmed.com).

Yeah, *Mommy*, how 'bout you stop causing me fungal infections (whatever those are)?!

TOYS

If my middle name was a dollar sign like his, I'd think I was the Richie Rich of Dog Toy Land. Ten toy boxes! With at least ten toys per box! With boxes all around the house (equidistant from one another thanks to the perfect PD route I set up during the home renovation)! Too bad I'm anti-costume or I'd consider donning Richie's waistcoat, white shirt with

Eton collar, giant red bow tie, and blue shorts. No thanks. I'm already covered in toys!

And it's great! It's like Mommy now runs FAO Schwarz or something. I don't do alcohol (which as you know was banned when I took over the shopping list and tossed it with other toxic-to-dog food and beverages), but I am guessing it's accurate to say I'm positively drunk on toys!

TOYS REALITY

And now here comes some research to rain right on my March of the Toys Parade—which, I learned, is an actual annual event in Ball Ground, Georgia!

Well, I have to be honest here. Most of the toy research is in our playtime favor. Almost every site says not only is it up to the human (and based on what they can handle and afford), but that dog *need* toys. Phew!

"For dogs and other pets, toys are not a luxury, but a necessity," says Humanesociety.org, adding this: "Toys are important to your dog's well-being. Toys help fight boredom when you have to leave your dog at home, and provide comfort when they're feeling nervous. Toys can even help prevent your dog from developing certain problem behaviors."

Some are kinda good news/kinda bad news. Like this: "It doesn't matter if your dogs have ten toys or one hundred; the key is limiting accessibility. Too many handy toys create indifference and negate their purpose" (dailypuppy.com).

Um. No. Their purpose is to make us dogs happy and for us to access which toys we want and when we want them! Right?

This site starts off bad: "It's better to have a few toys used well than a lot of toys not used at all" (vetstreet.com).

Which is truly none of their bees (or even PD ear) wax because I *do* use them all; it just takes a while to get to all one hundred plus. I am sure this is the case at your home-cum-toy store as well.

But it ends kinda good: Toys "redirect your dogs' natural chewing (and) eliminate any possibility of boredom" (Vetstreet.com).

And some sites say toys quell anxiety and also calm us when our humans are out doing whatever it is humans are doing out there that doesn't involve walkies and buying us treats and kibble and going to the dog park.

And finally there are just a little (*thankfully very few) downright dumb, er, I mean, bad news online:* "A good rule of thumb is about *10-15 toys* (italics PD's) which are swapped and changed around at regular intervals, giving your dog plenty of variety," says petsrader.com, whose piece goes on to make things worse by adding: "You might find that as they get older, your dog needs fewer toys than when they were a puppy..."

I'm just going to stop researching here because things are going downhill as fast as my dogsled holding my Kong Supreme and Fluff and Tuff Ball and Outward Hound Dog Tornado Puzzle (and maybe a couple of other things).

COSTUMES:

I get why humans say, "I workout to look good naked." Because I look super good naked and not wearing stupid costumes. I'm like that naked guy in that old Ray Stevens' song "The Streak," just racing around naked. Naked as the day I was born, a jaybird, buck naked, without a stitch, in the raw, in my birthday suit, in the buff, and in the altogether! Yep, wearing "nothing but a smile" since I shredded and otherwise rid our household of all dogwear.

COSTUMES REALITY:

Most everything I found online says putting us in Wonder Woman and Aquaman outfits is not earning our humans superhero status in the opinions of most of us; it's not the end of the world—unless it's constraining or otherwise unsafe (too loose, flammable, etc.).

But most dogs I know don't want to be the Taco Bell dog or Santa's reindog. The sites say mostly stuff like this: "A photo of a happy dog wearing a bandanna is better than one of a stressed dog in a full body elf suit" (offtheleash.com.au).

But maybe my shredding got a wee bit out of hand. Maybe I forgot about this thing God made called "seasons." It's not always pretty out. There's rain and sleet and snow and other mailman-phrase stuff out there. And I hate to admit that a lot of sites say that during foul weather—mainly very cold weather—we would benefit from wearing a cover up, like a coat, when temperatures dip into the freezing zone. And some humans put a raincoat on dogs when it's raining out, but cold weather seems to be the main concern.

So . . .okay, I'll only rip up Frankenstein suits and St. Patrick's Day red beards and Einstein white wigs and Theory of Relativity ties and . . . well, most everything else but a couple of jackets. And maybe one pair of fur-lined Prada booties. But that's it.

HOME RENOVATION

Just never mind. Not worth reliving now that things have gone so far off the rails.

HOME RENOVATION REALITY

I told you Mommy is on the floor in a ball. You already know how my PD-as-foreman-of-the-home-redo turned into PD-the-wrecking-ball-ruiner-of-everything-that-was-happy turned out. If your human looks as catatonic as my Mommy does right now, I know you likely are licking their crying or frozen face too.

Which brings us back to our kitchen floor. The kitchen floor to which Mommy used to toss treats and over which she would waggle my (plenty of) toys in front of my happy pug face. And which now has a Mommy kitten-in-a-ball mewling.

And I am so so so sad.

And I also am so so so bad. Mommy says never call your dog bad. But there is just no other word for all I've caused. And I meant so well.

What I couldn't figure at first, though, is why I was so affected by Mommy's tears? I mean, I got what I wanted. PD won! The victor! Prince of the house and the walk and everything everything everything.

But I am not a victor. And now I know why.

I did a lot of research for this manual. But you know what my favorite part of all my research was?

I learned why Mommy's lying on our floor sobbing made me want to sob too. And maybe right now—a couple months after you, too, have come away in the reprogramming of your human and transformation of your life and greatly advanced in your journey from servant to master—your human is on the floor weeping and you want to weep too.

I feel this way because Mommy is *Mommy*. She is my whole heart. And when she is sad, I am sad. And so of course I'm weeping and you probably are too.

As if we need the reassurance we are right:

Healthypawpetinsurance.com was asked if dogs see humans as their parents and their response has me all smiley and plus my eyes are a little wet for some strange reason...

"So, yes, a puppy can definitely think of you as his 'mother'— that is, his provider and protector—and develop as strong an emotional bond with you as if you were blood-related. Your puppy will also quickly learn to pick you out among strangers, both by sight and through his powerful sense of smell" (healthypawspetinsurance.com).

And this from mic.com: "Not only do dogs seem to love us back, they actually see us as their family. It turns out that dogs rely on humans more than they do their own kind for affection, protection and everything in between."

Doggysaurus.com adds: "The scientists were able to show that dogs were much more confident and self-assured when in the presence of their owners, just like the kids are. In other words, the dog owner acted as a safety net and security for the dog."

And: "Dogs interact with their human caregivers in the same way babies do their parents. When dogs are scared or worried, they run to their owners, just as distressed toddlers make a beeline for their parents."

And seeing Mommy crying on the floor is making me scared and me worried and me stressed. And that's why I made that same beeline to Mommy and lick-lick-licked her face and now it's me who's distressed because it didn't seem to help.

So now I am on the floor spooning against her and howling my own cry. And crying and crying with Mommy. Because I did this. I caused all of this. I thought I was making things all better and I wasn't making anything better. Except for me. And for you.

But not for Mommy. Not for your human. They are sad. Everything is topsy turvy terrible.

Because you know what? Much as I want all the food I can stuff in my treat hole; and every toy from Dog Toys 'R' Us; and to have my way at the dog park by blowing up all regulations; and to govern walkies as to pace and time length and where I wee and poopie; and to never be forced to go to the icky groomer; and even to have total say into how our very house is laid out . . . well, you know what?

The Zen I thought we all were reaching was an illusion.

The paradise I thought we'd attained was purgatory; the El Dorado was a stale Dorito; our Shangri-La was Sheol; the "chill" we all were feeling was hellfire!

Getting happiness for *me me me* just ended in *misery misery misery*. And I can feel the wind from your collective tails wagging in sad agreement.

Because you know what? True peace with our humans is just like their true peace with one another. The dog/human partnership only works well if there is mutual love and respect. I was loving me and you were loving you and we were having a grand ol' time fetching after everything our slobbering-with-greed dog hearts lusted for, but...

We forgot that one party's victory has to mean the other party's loss. And that's fine when I once again beat Ralph at marking trees or yank him over at an imagined game of tug-of war or send him a physic stink eye if I envision he is even considering approaching my fawn girl crush. But this is different.

This is our human. This is our caregiver. Our chauffeur, chef, walk-giver, medicine-from-vet dispenser, toy-buyer, treat-bestower, warm coat–provider, even . . . yes . . . tooth decay–preventer. And so much more. More than would fill a whole chapter. A whole book.

More than fills my whole heart.

I was wrong. Just so wrong. But you know what? I know it was a roundabout way through the maze but at the other end we all earned a great treat from this training manual. And it's this:

While we have been busy training our humans to behave the way we wanted, we learned it wasn't what we wanted at all. Getting our way at their expense sounds great until reality hits and your whole world is upside down and you're sad down to your very soul because you hurt Mommy (or Daddy).

I love being stinky and buried in toys and treats and running the show and all the rest. Until it occurs to me that I have turned into Pugzilla and am causing more physical and emotional destruction than any prehistoric sea monster awakened and empowered by nuclear radiation ever dreamed of. Who needs a reptilian monster when you have a PD monster? And you monster. And all of us furry monsters wreaking havoc throughout the land.

So. Turns out our final lesson was not the home renovation.

Our final lesson is that sometimes having your whole world collapse can be a good thing. Because we learned that in the end, we were the ones being trained on how to treat them:

With kindness;

With respect;

With minding our manners (well, to the extent mutts are "mannered");

With not being gluttonous (well, at least not howling like starved wolves when dinner is over);

With recognizing we have different tastes in decor (but I will never get these sconce thingies);

With considering donning those moronic patent leather red booties (don't go there) when there's snow;

With not having to run the whole house, walkie, park, show;

Basically with not having a one-sided relationship with our humans that only has us winning and only has them losing.

Now, we won't get this perfect. We *are* dogs, after all. But thanks to your Alpha PD, you—and okay, me—did learn a super good lesson in what matters most: The bond between dogs and their humans, humans and their dogs. We learned the only way to get along in this human-and-dog companion world is as a team, respectively, side by side.

Respect for our humans and their humane treatment of us well-trained happy dogs.

So this ended up being a pretty great training manual after all!

You know, once in a while I see Mommy fall apart. Okay, I've seen it a bunch of times. But mostly having a really rough workday or burning dinner again or getting sad news, or getting sad-to-her news like missing a Nordstrom sale. But I never witnessed what I did today; I never saw Mommy fall completely to pieces over what I caused, what I did. And I know you are on the floor with your human, your whole heart shattered and feeling just the same.

But hooray! We get to make it all better! Today a big face lick, tomorrow a big bully stick . . . in our fat stuffy bed, in our home restored to its former perfection (with sconces and everything). And our relationship with our human restored too, to the way God designed it: Humans training dogs . . . on how to get along with humane humans. Round and round like happy PD chasing his tail.

THE END

Oh! PS: No refunds, though! I had expenses! You signed up at your own risk! (And I should have charged Ralph double in the first place.)

GET IN TOUCH WITH PD!

You can write to him at

PD The Pug Productions
2200 Wilson Boulevard
Suite 102-265
Arlington, VA 22201

Or give him a shout at

PDthePug@gmail.com

ABOUT THE AUTHOR

PD the Pug's 2021 debut book, *Get Me Out Of Here! Reflections of PD the Put-Upon Pug* launched the writing career of the world's favorite "misunderstood" dog whose attempts to set things right tend not to quite go to plan.

While he awaits the day that he is named first-ever canine winner of the esteemed Pulitzer for his prose, he does have an impressive resume for such a young pug.

Among his many accomplishments, PD holds a certification of achievement for passing Puppy One training class. He additionally holds the record for most tail-chasing spins in one go, is distinguished as the preeminent dog park hole digger two years running, and is unequalled in the ability to recognize dog breeds by the smell of their rumps while blindfolded. As a puppy he won the highly coveted Pee Award for tipping over while urinating against a bush.

This descendent of a breed that once was the treasured companion to Chinese royalty somehow finds himself living in Arlington, VA, with silly but beloved Mommy.

You can visit PD online at PDThePugProductions.com and get in touch with him at pdthepug@gmail.com.

No, You Sit! is his second book.

ABOUT MOMMY

Mommy Marilee Joyce lives with PD the Pug in his Arlington home. She has the privilege of feeding, walking, and bathing him; getting the goopies out of his googly eyes; cleaning up his whoopsies; Q-tipping his ears and nose fold; and explaining that it is merely his reflection he is barking at in the sliding glass door and not a threat to the household, his toys, or his treats.

Marilee is the owner of Joyce Communications in Washington, DC and PD The Pug Productions. She is a former anchor and reporter for several television affiliates. In Washington, she has produced and hosted several television programs from Capitol Hill, and her company offers full video and audio production services.

Mommy is amazed anew with each sunrise that she lives with such a brainy dog. She hears he is working on his third book...

OTHER WORKS BY PD THE PUG

Get Me Out of Here! Reflections of PD the Put-Upon Pug